Birds and Poets, with Other Papers

John Burroughs

Contents

BIRDS AND POETS..7
TOUCHES OF NATURE. 41
    I..41
    II...44
    III..45
    IV. 47
    V..47
    VI. 48
    VII..50
    VIII. 51
    IX...52
    X...53
    XII..55
    XIII...56
    XIV...57
    XVI...58
    XVII. 58
A BIRD MEDLEY. 61
APRIL. 75
SPRING POEMS. 83
OUR RURAL DIVINITY. 90
BEFORE GENIUS. 105
EMERSON..117
    I. 117
    II..126
THE FLIGHT OF THE EAGLE. 133
TO WALT WHITMAN. 133
THE FLIGHT OF THE EAGLE. 133

BIRDS AND POETS, WITH OTHER PAPERS

BY

John Burroughs

BIRDS AND POETS.

" In summer, when the shawes be shene,
And leaves be large and long, It is full merry in fair forest
To hear the fowlès' song. The wood-wele sang, and wolde not cease,
Sitting upon the spray ; So loud, it wakened Robin Hood
In the greenwood where he lay."

IT might almost be said that the birds are J all birds of the poets and of no one else, because it is only the poetical temperament that fully responds to them. So true is this, that all the great ornithologists—original namers and biographers of the birds— have been poets in deed, if not in word. Audubon is a notable case in point, who, if he had not the tongue or pen of the poet, certainly had the eye and ear and heart— "the fluid and attaching character" and the singleness of purpose, the enthusiasm, the unworldliness, the love, that characterises the true and divine race of bards.

So had Wilson, though perhaps not in as large a measure ; yet he took fire as only a poet can. While making a journey on foot to Philadelphia, shortly after landing in this country, he caught sight of the red-headed woodpecker flitting among the trees a bird that shows like a tricoloured scarf among the foliage, and it so kindled his enthusiasm that his life was devoted to the pursuit of the birds from that day. It was a lucky hit. Wilson had already set up as a poet in Scotland, and was still fermenting when the bird met his eye and suggested to his soul a new outlet for its enthusiasm.

The very idea of a bird is a symbol and a suggestion to the poet. J A bird seems to be at the top of the scale so vehement and intense is his life large brained, large lunged, hot, ecstatic, his frame charged with buoyancy and his heart with song. The beautiful vagabonds, endowed with every grace, masters of all climes, and knowing no bounds, show many human aspirations are I realised in their free, holiday-lives—and how I many suggestions to the poet in their flight and song

Indeed is not the bird the original type and teacher of the poet, and do we not demand of the human lark or thrush that he "shake out his carols " in the same free and spontaneous manner as his winged prototype ? Kingsley has shown how surely the old minnesingers and early ballad-writers have learned of the birds, taking their key-note from the blackbird, or the wood-lark, or the throstle, and giving utterance to a melody as simple and unstudied. Such things as the following were surely caught from the fields or the woods :—

" She sat down below a thorn,
Fine flowers in the valley,
And there has she her sweet babe born,
And the green leaves they grow rarely."

Or the best lyric pieces, how like they are to certain bird-songs,—clear, ringing, ecstatic, and suggesting that challenge and triumph which the outpouring of the male bird contains. (Is not the genuine singing, lyrical quality essentially masculine ?) Keats and Shelley, perhaps, more notably than any other English poets, have the bird-organisation and the piercing wild-bird cry. This of course is not saying that they are the greatest poets, but that they have pre-eminently the sharp semi-tones of the sparrows and larks.

But when the general reader thinks of the birds of the poets he very naturally calls to!mind the renowned birds, the lark and nightingale, Old-World melodists, embalmed in Old-World poetry, but occasionally appearing on these shores, transported in the verse of some callow singer. The very oldest poets, the towering antique bards, seem to make little mention of the song-birds. They loved better the soar-ling, swooping birds of prey, the eagle, the ominous birds, the vultures, the storks, and cranes, or the clamorous sea-birds and the screaming hawks. These suited better the rugged, warlike character of the times and the simple, powerful souls of the singers themselves. Homer must have heard the twittering of the swallows, the cry of the plover, the voice of the turtle, and the warble of the nightingale; but they were not adequate symbols to express what he felt or to adorn his theme. Æschylus saw in the eagle " the dog of Jove," and his verse cuts like a sword with such a conception.

It is not because the old bards were less as poets, but that they were more as men. To strong, susceptible characters the music of nature is not confined to sweet sounds. The defiant scream of the hawk circling aloft, the wild whinny of the loon, the whooping of the crane, the booming of the bittern, the vulpine bark of the eagle, the loud trumpeting of the migratory geese sounding down out of the midnight sky; or by the sea-shore, the coast of New Jersey or Long Island, the wild crooning of the flocks of gulls, repeated, continued by the hour, swirling sharp and shrill, rising and falling like' the wind in a storm, as they circle above the beach, or dip to the dash of the waves —are much more welcome in certain moods than any and all mere bird-melodies, in keeping as they are with the shaggy and untamed features of ocean and woods, and suggesting something like the Richard Wagner music in the ornithological orchestra.

> " Nor these alone whose notes
> Nice-fingered art must emulate in vain,
> But cawing rooks, and kites that swim sublime
> In still repeated circles, screaming loud,
> The jay the pie, and even the boding owl,
> That hails the rising moon, have charms for me,"

says Cowper. "I never hear," says Burns in one of his letters, '-'the loud solitary whistle of the curlew in a summer noon, or the wild mixing cadence of a troop of grey plovers in an autumnal morning, without feeling an elevation of soul like the enthusiasm of devotion or poetry."

Even the Greek minor poets, the swarm of them that are represented in the Greek Anthology, rarely make affectionate mention of the birds, except perhaps Sappho, whom Ben Jonson makes speak of the nightingale as—

'' The dear glad angel of the spring."

The cicada, the locust, and the grasshopper, are often referred to, but rarely by name any of the common birds. That Greek ! grasshopper must have been a wonderful creature. He was a sacred object in Greece, and is spoken of by the poets as a charming songster. What we would say of birds the Greek said of this favourite insect. When Socrates and Phædrus came to the fountain shaded by the plane-tree, where they had their famous discourse, Socrates said, "Observe the freshness of the spot, how charming and very delightful it is, and how summer-like and shrill it sounds from the choir of grass hoppers. " One of the poets in the Anthology finds a grasshopper struggling in a spider's web, which he releases with the words—

" Go safe and free with your sweet voice of song."

Another one makes the insect say to a rustic who had captured him

"Me, the Nymphs' wayside minstrel whose sweet note
O'er sultry hill is heard, and shady grove to float."

Still another sings how a grasshopper took the place of a broken string on his lyre, and "filled the cadence due."

" For while six chords beneath my fingers cried, He with his tuneful voice the seventh supplied ;
The midday songster of the mountain set
His pastoral ditty to my canzonet;
And when he sang, his modulated throat
Accorded with the lifeless string I smote."

While we are trying to introduce the lark in this country, why not try this Pindaric grasshopper also ?

It is to the literary poets and to the minstrels of a softer age that we must look for special mention of the song-birds and for poetical rhapsodies upon them. The night. ingale is the most general favourite, ana nearly all the more noted English poets have sung her praises. To the melancholy poet she is melancholy, and to the cheerful she is cheerful. Shakespeare in one of his sonnets speaks of her song as mournful, while Martial calls her the "most garrulous " of birds. Milton sang—

" Sweet bird, that shunn'st the noise of folly,
Most musical, most melancholy,
Thee, chantress, oft the woods among
I woo, to hear thy evening song."

To Wordsworth she told another story-

 O nightingale! thou surely art
A creature of ebullient heart;
These notes of thine they pierce and pierce;
Tumultuous harmony and fierce !
Thou sing'st as if the god of wine
Had helped thee to a valentine ;
A song in mockery and despite
Of shades, and dews, and silent night,
And steady bliss, and all the loves
Now sleeping in these peaceful groves." •
In a like vein Coleridge sang—

" 'Tis the merry nightingale
That crowds and hurries and precipitates
With fast, thick warble his delicious notes."

Keats's poem on the nightingale is doubtless more in the spirit of the bird's strain than any other. It is less a description of the song and more the song itself. Hood called the nightingale "The sweet and plaintive Sappho of the dell."

I mention the nightingale only to point my remarks upon its American rival, the famous mocking-bird of the Southern States, which is also a nightingale a night-singer and which no doubt excels the Old-World bird in the variety and compass of its powers. The two birds belong to totally-distinct families, there being no American species which answers to the European nightingale, as there are that answer to the robin, the cuckoo, the blackbird, and numerous others. Philomel has the colour, manners, and habits of a thrush our hermit-thrush but it is not a thrush at all, but a warbler. I gather from the books that its song is protracted and full rather than melodious, — a capricious, long-continued warble, doubling and redoubling, rising and falling, issuing from the groves and the great gardens, and associated in the minds of the poets with love and moonlight and the privacy of sequestered walks. All our sympathies and attractions are with the bird, and we do not forget that Arabia and Persia are there back of its song.

Own nightingale has mainly the reputation of the! caged bird, and is famed mostly for its powers of mimicry, which are truly wonderful, enabling the bird to exactly reproduce and even improve upon the notes of almost any other songster. But in a state of freedom it has a song of its own which is infinitely rich and various. It is a garrulou polyglot when it chooses to be, and there a dash of the clown and the buffoon in ill nature which too often flavours its who performance, especially in captivity; but its native haunts, and when its love-passsiom is upon it, the serious and even grand of its character comes out. In Alabama Florida its song may be heard all tbr the sultry summer night, at times low air plaintive, then full and strong. A friond Thoreau and a careful observer, who he resided in Florida, tells me that this bird is a much more marvellous singer than it has the credit of being. He describes a habit it has of singing on the wing on moonlig' nights, that would be worth going

South hear. Starting from a low bush, it moun in the air, and continues its flight apparent to an altitude of several hundred feet, r maining on the wing a number of .miiaute and pouring out its song with -the utmo clearness and ***abandon*** a slowly risi musical rocket that fills the night air wi harmonious sounds. Here are both the la. . and nightingale in one; and ***if*** poets we as plentiful down South as they are in Ne England, we should have heard of this son long ago, and had it celebrated in apipopria . verse. But so far only one Southern poet, Wilde, has accredited the bird this song. This he has done in the following admirable sonnet—

" TO THE MOCKING-BIRD.
" Winged mimic of the woods ! thou motley fool,
Who shall thy gay buffoonery describe
Thine ever-ready notes of ridicule
Pursue thy fellows still with jest and gibe.
Wit— sophist—songster—Yorick of thy tribe,
Thou sportive satirist of Nature's school,
o thee the palm of scoffing we ascribe,
Arch scoffer, and mad Abbot of Misrule!
For such thou art by day—but all night long
Thou pour'st a soft, sweet, pensive, solemn strain,
As if thou didst in this, thy moonlight song,
Like to the melancholy Jacques, complain,
Musing on falsehood, violence, and wrong,
And sighing for thy motley coat again."

Aside from this sonnet, the mocking-bird has got into poetical literature, so far as I know, in only one notable instance, and that in the page of a poet where we would least expect to find him—a bard who habitually bends his ear only to the musical surge and rhythmus of total nature, and is as little wont to turn aside for any special beauties or points as the most austere of the ancient masters. I refer to Walt Whitman's "Out of the cradle endlessly rocking" in which the mocking-bird plays a part. The poet's treatment of the bird is entirely ideal, and eminently characteristic. That is to say, it is altogether poetical and not at all ornithological

; yet it contains a rendering or free translation of a bird-song—the nocturn of the mocking-bird, singing and calling through the night for its lost mate—that I consider quite unmatched in our literature.

" Once, Paumanok,
When the snows had melted, and the Fifth-month grass was growing,
Up this sea-shore, in some briers,
Two guests from Alabama—two together,
And their nest, and four light-green eggs, spotted with brown,
And every day the he-bird, to and fro, near at hand,
And every day the she-bird, crouched on her nest, silent, with bright eyes,
And every day I, a curious boy, never too close, never disturbing them,
Cautiously peering, absorbing, translating.

Shine I Shine I Shine I Pour down your warmth, great Sun I While we bask—we two together.
Two together I
Winds blow South, or winds blow North,
Day come white, or night come black,
Home, or rivers and mountains from home,
Singing all time, minding no time,
If we two but keep together.

Till of a sudden,
May be killed, unknown to her mate,
One forenoon the she-bird crouched not on the
nest,
Nor returned that afternoon, nor the next,
Nor ever appeared again.

And thenceforward, all summer, in the sound of the sea,
And at night, under the full of the moon, in calmer weather,
Over the hoarse surging of the sea,

Or flitting from brier to brier by day,
I saw, I heard at intervals, the remaining one,
the he-bird,
The solitary guest from Alabama.

Blow! blow! blow!
Blow up, sea-winds, along Paumanok's shore I
wait and I wait, till you blow my mate to me.

Yes, when the stars glistened,
All night long, on the prong of a moss-scalloped stake,
Down, almost amid the slapping waves,
Sat the lone singer, wonderful, causing tears.

He called on his mate:
He poured forth the meanings which I, of all men, know.

Soothe! soothe! soothe!
Close on Us wave soothes the wave behind,
And again another behind, embracing and lapping, every one close,
But my love soothes not me, not me.

Low hangs the moon—it rose late.
Oh it is lagging—oh I think it is heavy with love, with love.

Oh madly the sea pushes, pushes upon the land,
With love—with love.

O night! do I not see my love fluttering out there among the breakers.
What is that little black thing I see there in the white

Loud! loud! loud!

Loud I call to you, my love !
High and clear I shoot my voice over the waves;
Surely you must know who is here, is here ;
You must know who I am, my love.

Low hanging moon !
What is that dusky spot in your brown yellow ?
Oh it is the shape, the shape of my mate !
0 moon, do not keep her from me any longer.

Land I land I Oland I
Whichever way I turn, oh I think you could give
my mate back again, if you only would ;
For 1 am almost sure I see her dimly whicheverway I look.

0 rising stars I Perhaps the one I want so much will rise, will rise with some
of you.
O throat ! O trembling throat !
Sound clearer through the atmosphere !
Pierce the woods, the earth;
Somewhere listening to catch you, must be the one I want.

Shake out, carols !
Solitary here—the night's carols I
Carols of lonesome love t Death's carols !
Carols under that lagging, yellow, waning moon I
Oh, under that moon, where she droops almost down into the sea I
0 reckless, despairing carols.

Bui soft I sink low;
Soft I let me just murmur ;

And do you wait a moment, you husky-noised sea;
For somewhere 1 believe I heard my mate responding to me,
So faint I must be still, be still to listen ;
But not altogether still, for then she might not come immediately to me.

Hither, my love !
 Here I am I Here!
With this just-sustained note I announce myself to you;
This gentle call is for you, my love, for you.

Do not be decoyed elsewhere I
That is the whistle of the wind—it is not my voice;
That is the fluttering, the fluttering of the spray;
Those are the shadows of leaves.

O darkness ! Oh in vain !
Oh I am very sick and sorrowful."

The bird that occupies the second place to the nightingale in British poetical literature I is the skylark a pastoral bird as the Philo-mel is an arboreal,a creature of light and air and motion, the companion of the ploughman, the shepherd, the harvester,—whose nest is in the stubble and whose tryst is in the clouds. Its life affords that kind of contrast which the imagination loves—one moment a plain pedestrian bird, hardly distinguishable from the ground, the next a soaring, untiring songster, revelling in the upper air, challenging the eye to follow him and the ear to separate his notes.

The lark's song is not especially melodious, but lithesome, sibilant, and unceasing. Its type is the grass, where the bird makes its , home, abounding, multitudinous, the notes nearly all alike and all in the same key, but I rapid, swarming, prodigal, showering dowry as thick and fast as drops of rain in a summer shower.

Many noted poets have sung the praises of the lark or been kindled by his example. Shelley's ode, and Wordsworth's "To a Skylark," are well known to all readers of poetry, while every school-boy will recall Hogg's poem, beginning—

" Bird of the wilderness,
Blithesome and cumberless,
Sweet be thy matin o'er moorland and lea !
Emblem of happiness,
Blest is thy dwelling-place—
Oh to abide in the desert with thee !"

I heard of an enthusiastic American who went about English fields hunting a lark with Shelley's poem in his hand, thinking no doubt to use it as a kind of guide-book to the intricacies and harmonies of the song. He reported not having heard any larks, though I have little doubt they were soaring and singing about him all the time, though of course they did not sing to his ear the song that Shelley heard. The poets are the best natural historians, only yon must know-how to read them. They translate the facts largely and freely. A celebrated lady once said to Turner, "I confess, I cannot see in nature what you do." "Ah, madam," said the complacent artist, " don't you wish you could !"

Shelley's poem is perhaps better known and has a higher reputation among literary folk than Wordsworth's; it is more lyrical and lark-like; but it is needlessly long, though no longer than the lark's song itself, but the lark can't help it and Shelley can. I quote only a few stanzas :—

" In the golden lightning
Of the sunken sun,
O'er which clouds are bright'ning,
Thou dost float and run,
Like an unbodied joy whose race is just begun.

The pale purple even

Melts around thy flight;
Like a star of heaven,
In the broad daylight
Thou art unseen, but yet I hear thy shrill delight.

Keen as are the arrows
Of that silver sphere,
Whose intense lamp narrows
In the white dawn clear,
Until we hardly see, but feel that it is there.

All the earth and air
With thy voice is loud,
As, when night is bare,
From one lonely cloud
The moon rains out her beams, and heaven is overflowed.

"Wordsworth has written two poems upon the lark, in one of which he calls the bird "pilgrim of the sky." This is the one quoted by Emerson in "Parnassus." Here is the concluding stanza :—

"Leave to the nightingale her shady wood ;
A privacy of glorious light is thine,
Whence thou dost pour upon the world a flood
Of harmony, with instinct more divine;
Type of the wise, who soar, but never roam,
True to the kindred points of heaven and
home."

The other poem I give entire :—
"Up with me ! up with me, into the clouds !
For thy song, lark, is strong;
Up with me, up with me, into the clouds !

Singing, singing,
With all the heavens about thee ringing,
Lift me, guide me till I find
That spot which seems so to thy mind !
I have walked through wildernesses dreary,
And to-day my heart is weary;

Had I now the wings of a fairy
Up to thee would I fly.
There is madness about thee, and joy divine
In that song of thine ;

Up with me, up with me high and high
To thy banqueting-place in the sky !
Joyous as morning,
Thou art laughing and scorning,
Thou hast a nest for thy love and thy rest;
And, though little troubled with sloth,
Drunken lark ! thou wouldst be loth
To be such a traveller as I.
Happy, happy liver !
With a soul as strong as a mountain-river,
Pouring out praise to th' Almighty Giver,
Joy and jollity be with us both !
Hearing thee, or else some other,
As merry a brother,
I on earth will go plodding on,
By myself, cheerfully, till the day is done."

But better than either—better and more than a hundred pages—is Shake-speare's simple line—

"Hark, hark, the lark at heaven's gate sings," or John Lyly's, his contemporary—

" Who is't now we hear ?
None but the lark so shrill and clear;
Now at heaven's gate she claps her wings,
The morn not waking till she sings."

We have no well-known pastoral bird in the Eastern States that answers to the skylark. The American pipit or titlark and the shore-lark, both birds of the far North, and seen in the States only in fall and winter, belong to this species, and are said to sing on the wing in a similar strain. Common enough in our woods are two birds that have many of the habits and manners of the lark—the water-thrush and the golden-l crowned thrush, or oven-bird. • They are both walkers, and the latter frequently sings on the wing up aloft after the manner of the lark. Starting from its low perch, it rises in a spiral flight far above the tallest trees, and breaks out in a clear, ringing, ecstatic song, sweeter and more richly modulated than the skylark's, but brief, ceasing almost before you have noticed it; whereas the skylark goes singing away after you have forgotten him and returned to him half a dozen times.

But in the West, in Dakota, and along the Platte and Yellowstone rivers, it seems we have a genuine skylark (Sprague's lark), an excelsior songster, that from far up in the transparent blue rains down its notes for many minuses together. It is probably a lineal descendant of the European species, and is, no doubt, destined to figure in the future poetical literature of the Yellowstone. Throughout the northern and eastern I parts of the Union the lark would find a dangerous rival in the bobolink, a bird that has no European prototype, and no near relatives anywhere— standing quite alone, unique, and, in the qualities of hilarity and musical tintinnabulation, with a song unequalled. He has already a secure place in general literature, having been laureated by a no less poet than Bryant, and invested with a lasting human charm in the sunny page of Irving,—and is the only one of our songsters, I believe, the mocking-bird cannot parody or imitate. He affords the most marked example of exuberant pride, and a glad, rollicking, holiday spirit, that can be seen among our birds. Every note expresses complacency and glee. He is a beau of the first pattern, and, unlike any other bird of my acquaintance, pushes his gallantry to the point of wheeling gaily into the train of every female that comes along, even after the season of courtship is over and the matches all settled; and when she leads him on too wild a chase, he turns lightly about and breaks out with a song that is ' precisely analogous to a burst of gay and self-satisfied laughter, as much as to say, " ***Ha! ha! ha! I must have my fun, Miss Silverthimble, thimble, thimble, if I break every heart in the meadow, see, see, see ! "***.

At the approach of the breeding season the bobolink undergoes a complete change; his form changes, his colour changes, his flight changes. From mottled brown or brindle he becomes black and white, earning, in some localities, the shocking name of "skunk bird;" his small, compact form becomes broad and conspicuous, and his ordinary flight is laid aside for a mincing, affected gait, in which he seems to use only the very tips of his wings. It is very noticeable what a contrast he presents to his mate at this season, not only in colour but in manners, she being as shy and retiring as he is forward and hilarious. Indeed she seems disagreeably serious and indisposed to any fun or jollity, skurrying away at his approach, and apparently annoyed at every endearing word and look. It is surprising that all this parade of plumage and tinkling of cymbals should be gone through with and persisted in to, please a creature so coldly indifferent as she really seems to be. If Robert O'Lincoln has been stimulated into acquiring this holiday uniform and this musical gift by the approbation of Mrs. Robert, as Darwin, with his sexual selection principle would have us believe, then there must have been a time when the females of this tribe were not quite so chary of their favours as they are now. Indeed, I never knew a female bird of any kind that did not appear utterly indifferent to the charms of voice and plumage that the male birds are so fond of displaying. But I am inclined to believe ' that the males think only of themselves and . of outshining each other, and not at all of the approbation of their mates, as, in an analogous case in a higher species, it is well known who the fema les dress for and whom they want to kill with envy !

I know of no other song-bird that expresses so much self-consciousness and vanity, and comes so near being an ornithological coxcomb. The red-bird, the yellow-bird, the indigo-bird, the oriole, the cardinal grosbeak and others all birds of brilliant plumage and musical ability, seem quite unconscious of self, and neither by tone nor act challenge the admiration of the beholder.

By the time the bobolink reaches the Potomac, in September, he has degenerated into a game-bird that is slaughtered by tens of thousands in the marshes. I think the prospects now are of his gradual extermination, as gunners and sportsmen are clearly on the increase, while the limit of the bird's productivity in the North has no doubt been reached long ago. There are no more meadows to be added to his domain there, while he is being waylaid and cut off more and more on his return to the South. It is gourmand eat gourmand, until in half a century more I expect the blithest and merriest of our meadow songsters will have disappeared before the rapacity of human throats. But the poets have had a shot at him in good time, and have preserved some of his traits. Bryant's poem on this subject does not compare with his lines "To a Water-fowl,"—a subject so well suited to the peculiar, simple, and deliberate motion of his mind ; at the same time it is fit that the poet who sings of ."The Planting of the Apple-tree," should render into words the song of "Robert of Lincoln." I subjoin a few stanzas:—

"ROBERT OF LINCOLN.
" Merrily swinging on brier and weed,
Near to the neat of his little dame,
Over the mountain-side or mead,
Robert of Lincoln is telling his name:

Bob-o'-link, bob-o'-link,
Spink, spank, spink:
Snug and safe is that nest of ours,
Hidden among the summer flowers.
Chee, chee, chee.

Robert of Lincoln is gaily drest,
Wearing a bright black wedding-coat,

White are his shoulders and white his crest,
Hear him call in his merry note:
Bob-o'-link, bob-o'-link,
Spink, spank, spink:
Look what a nice new coat is mine,
Sure there was never a bird so fine.
Chee, chee, chee.

Robert of Lincoln's Quaker wife,
Pretty and quiet, with plain brown wings,
Passing at home a patient life,
Broods in the grass while her husband sings:
Bob-o'-link, bob-o'-link,
Spink, spank, spink:
Brood, kind creature; you need not fear
Thieves and robbers while I am here.
Chee, chee, chee."

But it has been reserved for' a practical ornithologist, Mr. Wilson Flagg, to write by far the best poem on the bobolink that I have yet seen. It is much more in the mood and spirit of the actual song than Byrant's poem.

"THE O'LINCOLN FAMILY.
" A flock of merry singing-birds were sporting in the grove;
Some were warbling cheerily, and some were making love:
There were Bobolincon, Wadolincon, Winter-seeble, Conquedle,—
A livelier set was never led by tabor, pipe, or fiddle,
Crying, 'Phew, shew, Wadolincon, see, see, Bobolincon,
Down among the tickletops, hiding in the buttercups !
I know the saucy chap, I see his shining cap
Bobbing in the clover there—see, see, see!'

Up flies Bobolincon, perching on an apple-tree,

Startled by his rival's song, quickened by his raillery,
Soon he spies the rogue afloat, curveting in the air,
And merrily he turns about, and warns him to beware!
Tis you that would a-wooing go, down among the rushes 0 !
But wait a week, till flowers are cheery,—wait a week, and ere you marry,
Be sure of a house wherein to tarry !
Wadolink, Whiskodink, Tom Denny, wait,
wait, wait
Every one 's a funny fellow; every one's a little mellow;
Follow, follow, follow, follow, o'er the hill and in the hollow!
Merrily, merrily, there they hie; now they rise and now they fly ;
They cross and turn, and in and out, and down in the middle, and wheel about,—
With a 'Phew, shew, Wadolincon! listen to me, Boholincon !
Happy's the wooing that 's speedily doing, that 's speedily doing,
That's merry and over with the bloom of the clover!
Bobolincon, Wadolincon, Winterseeble, follow, follow me!'"

Many persons, I presume, have admired 1 Wordsworth's poem on the cuckoo, with- out recognising its truthfulness, or how thoroughly, in the main, the description applies to our own species. If the poem had been written in New England or New York, it could not have suited our case better.

" 0 blithe new-comer! I have heard,
I hear thee and rejoice:
0 cuckoo! shall I call thee bird,
Or but a wandering voice ?

While I am lying on the grass,
Thy loud note smites my ear !
From hill to hill it seems to pass,
At once far off and near.

I hear thee babbling to the vale
Of sunshine and of flowers;
And unto me thou bring'st a tale
Of visionary hours.

Thrice welcome, darling of the spring !
Even yet thou art to me No bird, but an invisible thing,
A voice, a mystery.
The same whom in my school-boy days
I listened to ; the cry
Which made me look a thousand ways
In bush, and tree, and sky.

To seek thee did I often rove
Through woods and on the green;
And thou wert still a hope, a love;
Still longed for, never seen!

And I can listen to thee yet;
Can lie upon the plain
And listen, till I do beget
That golden time again.

0 blessed bird ! the earth we pace
Again appears to be
An unsubstantial, fairy place,
That is fit home for thee !"

Logan's stanzas, "To the Cuckoo," have less merit both as poetry and natural history, but they are older, and doubtless the later poet benefited by them. Burke admired them so much that while on a visit to Edinburgh he sought the author out to compliment him.

" Hail, beauteous stranger of the grove!
Thou messenger of spring!
Now Heaven repairs thy rural seat,
And woods thy welcome sing.

What time the daisy decks the green,
Thy certain voice we hear;
Hast thou a star to guide thy path,
Or mark the rolling year ?.

The school-boy, wandering through the wood
To pull the primrose gay,
Starts thy curious voice to hear,
And imitates thy lay.

Sweet bird ! thy bower is ever green,
Thy sky is ever clear;
Thou hast no sorrow in thy song,
No winter in thy year."

The European cuckoo is evidently a much gayer bird than ours, and much more noticeable.

" Hark, how the jolly cuckoos sing
' Cuckoo !' to welcome in the spring,"

says John Lyly, three hundred years agone. Its note is easily imitated, and boys will ; render it so perfectly as to deceive any but the shrewdest ear. An English lady tells , me its voice reminds you of children at play, and is full of gaiety and happiness. It is a persistent songster, and keeps up its call from morning to night. Indeed, certain parts of Wordsworth's poem—those that refer to the bird as a mystery, a wandering solitary voice—seem to fit our bird better than the European species. Our cuckoo is in fact a solitary wanderer, repeating its loud, guttural call in the depths of the forest, and well calculated to arrest the attention of a poet like Wordsworth, who was himself a kind of cuckoo, a solitary voice, syllabling the loneliness that broods over streams and woods :—

" At once far off and near."

Our cuckoo is not a spring bird, being seldom seen or heard in the North before June. He is a great devourer of canker-worms, and when these pests appear he comes out of his forest seclusion and makes excursions through the orchard stealthily and quietly, regaling himself upon those ! pulpy, fuzzy tidbits. His coat of deep cinnamon brown has a silky gloss and is very beautiful. His note or call is not musical, but loud, and has in a remarkable degree the quality of remoteness and introverted- I ness. It is like a vocal legend, and to the farmer bodes rain.

It is worthy of note, and illustrates some (things said further back, that birds not strictly denominated songsters but criers, | like the cuckoo, have been quite as great ' favourites with the poets and received as affectionate, treatment at their hands as the song-birds. One readily recalls Emerson's "Titmouse," Trowbridge's "Pewee," Celia Thaxter's " Sandpiper," and others of a like character.

It is also worthy of note that the owl appears to be a greater favourite with the poets than the proud soaring hawk. The owl is doubtless the more human and picturesque bird; then he belongs to the night and its weird effects. Bird of the silent wing and expansive eye, grimalkin in feathers, feline, mousing, haunting ruins and towers, and mocking the midnight stillness with thy uncanny cry ! The owl is the great bug-a-boo of the feathered tribes. His appearance by day is hailed by shouts of alarm and derision from nearly every bird that flies, from crows down to sparrows. They swarm about him like flies, and literally mob him back into his dusky retreat. Silence is as the breath of his nostrils to him, and the uproar that greets him when he emerges into the open day seems to alarm and confuse him as it does the pickpocket when everybody cries Thief.

But the poets, I say, have not despised him.

" The lark is but a bumpkin fowl;
He sleeps in his nest till morn ;
But my blessing upon the jolly owl
That all night blows his horn."

Both Shakespeare and Tennyson have made songs about him. This is Shakespeare's, from "Love's Labour's Lost,"and perhaps has reference to the white or snowy owl:

" When icicles hang by the wall,
And Dick the shepherd blows his nail,
And Tom bears logs into the hall,
And milk comes frozen home in pail;
When blood is nipped, and ways be foul,
Then nightly sings the staring owl,
Tu-who !
Tu-whit! tu-who! a merry note,
While greasy Joan doth keel the pot.
When all aloud the wind doth blow,
And coughing drowns the parson's saw,
And birds sit brooding in the snow,
And Marian's nose looks red and raw;
When roasted crabs hiss in the bowl,
Then nightly sings the staring owl,
Tu-who !
 Tu-whit! tu-who ! a merry note,
While greasy Joan doth keel the pot."

There is, perhaps, a slight reminiscence of this song in Tennyson's " Owl:"—

" When cats run home and light is come,
And dew is cold upon the ground,
And the far-off stream is dumb,
And the whirring sail goes round,
And the whirring sail goes round;
Alone and warming his five wits
The white owl in the belfry sits.

When merry milkmaids click the latch,
And rarely smells the new-mown hay,
And the cock hath sung beneath the thatch,
Twice or thrice his roundelay,
Twice or thrice his roundelay;
Alone and warming his five wits,
The white owl in the belfry sits."

Tennyson has not directly celebrated any of the more famous birds, but his poems contain frequent allusion to them. The " Wild bird, whose warble, liquid sweet, Kings Eden through the budded quicks, Oh, tell me where the senses mix, Oh, tell me where the passions meet,"—

of "In Memoriam," is doubtless the nightingale. And here we have the lark :—

" Now sings the woodland loud and long,
And distance takes a lovelier hue,
And drowned in yonder living blue
The lark becomes a sightless song."

And again in this from " A Dream of Fair Women :"—

"Then I heard A noise of some one coming through the lawn, And singing clearer than the crested bird That claps his wings at dawn."

The swallow is a favourite bird with I Tennyson, and is frequently mentioned, I beside being the principal figure in one of | those charming love-songs in " The Princess." His allusions to the birds, as to any other natural feature, show him to be a careful Observer, as when he speaks of

"The swamp, where hums the dropping snipe."

His single bird-poem, aside from the song I have quoted, is "The Blackbird," the Old-World prototype of our robin, as if our bird had doffed the aristocratic black for a more democratic suit on reaching these shores. In curious contrast to the colour of its plumage is its beak, which is as yellow as a kernel of Indian corn. The following are the two middle stanzas of the poem :—

" Yet though I spared thee all the spring,
Thy sole delight is, sitting still,
With that gold dagger of thy bill
To fret the summer jenneting.

A golden bill! the silver tongue,
Cold February loved, is dry;
Plenty corrupts the melody
That made thee famous once, when young."

Shakespeare, in one of his songs, alludes to the blackbird as the ouzel-cock; indeed he puts quite a flock of birds in this song :—

" The ouzel-cock so black of hue,
With orange-tawny bill;
The throstle with his note so true,
The wren with little quill;

The finch, the sparrow, and the lark,
The plain-song cuckoo grey, Whose note fall many a man doth mark,
And dares not answer nay."

So far as external appearances are concerned—form, plumage, grace of manner, etc., no tone ever had a less promising subject than had Trowbridge in the" Pewee." This , bird, if not the plainest dressed, is the most unshapely in the woods. It is stiff and abrupt in its manners and sedentary in its habits, sitting around all day, in the dark recesses of the woods, on the dry twigs and branches, uttering now and then its plaintive cry, and "with many a flirt and flutter" snapping up its insect game.

The pewee belongs to quite a large family 'of birds, all of whom have strong family traits, and who are not the most peaceable and harmonious of the sylvan folk. They are pugnacious, harsh voiced, angular in form and movement, with flexible tails and broad, flat, bristling beaks that stand to the face at the angle of a turn-up nose, and most of them wear a black cap pulled well down over their eyes. Their heads are large, neck and legs short, and elbows sharp. The wild Irishman of them all is the great-crested flycatcher, a large leather-coloured or sandy-complexioned bird that prowls through the woods, uttering its harsh, uncanny note and waging fierce warfare upon its fellows.

The exquisite of the species, and the braggart of the orchard, is the kingbird, a bully that loves to strap the feathers off its ! more timid neighbours like the bluebird, that feeds on the stingless bees of the hive, the drones, and earns the reputation of great boldness by teasing large hawks, while it gives a wide berth to little ones.

The best beloved of them all is the phoebe-bird, one of the firstlings of the spring, of whom so many of our poets have made [affectionate mention.

The wood-pewee is the sweetest voiced, and notwithstanding the ungracious things I have said of it, and of its relations, merits to the full all Trowbridge's pleasant fancies. His poem is indeed a very careful study of the bird and its haunts, and is good poetry as well as good ornithology.

" The listening Dryads hushed the woods;
The boughs were thick, and thin and few
The golden ribbons fluttered through;
Their sun-embroidered leafy hoods
The lindens lifted to the blue;
Only a little forest-brook;
The furthest hem of silence shook;
When in the hollow shades I heard,—
Was it a spirit or a bird ?
Or, strayed from Eden, desolate,
Some Peri calling to her mate,
Whom nevermore her mate would cheer ?
' Pe-ri! pe-ri! peer !
To trace it in its green retreat
I sought among the boughs in vain ;
And followed still the wandering strain,
So melancholy and so sweet,
The dim-eyed violets yearned with pain,
Twas now a sorrow in the air,
Some nymph's immortalised despair
Haunting the woods and waterfalls;
And now, at long, sad intervals,
Sitting unseen in dusky shade,
His plaintive pipe some fairy played,
With long-drawn cadence thin and clear,—
'Pe-wee! pe-wee! peer!'

Long-drawn and clear its closes were—
As if the hand of Music through
The sombre robe of Silence drew
A thread of golden gossamer;
So pure a flute the fairy blew
Like beggared princes of the wood,

In silver rags the birches stood;
The hemlocks, lordly counsellors,
Were dumb; the sturdy servitors,
In beechen jackets patched and grey,
Seemed waiting spell-bound all the day
That low, entrancing note to hear,—
'Pe-wee! pe-wee! peer!

I quit the search, and sat me down
"J Beside the brook, irresolute,
And watched a little bird in suit
Of sombre olive, soft and brown,
Perched in the maple branches, mute;
With greenish gold its vest was fringed,
Its tiny cap was ebon-tinged,
With ivory pale its wings were barred,
And its dark eyes were tender-starred.
'Dear bird I said, ' what is thy name ?
And thrice the mournful answer came,
So faint and far, and yet so near,—
Pe-wee! pe-wee! peer !

For so I found my forest bird,—
The pewee of the loneliest woods,
Sole singer in these solitudes,
Which never robin's whistle stirred,
Where never bluebird's plume intrudes.
Quick darting through the dewy morn,
The redstart trilled his twittering horn
And vanished in thick boughs; at even
Like liquid pearls fresh showered from heaven,
The high notes of the lone wood-thrush
Fell on the forest's holy hush;

But thou all day complainest here,—
'Pe-wee! pe-wee! peer!'"

Emerson's best natural history poem is ' the "Humblebee"—a poem as good in its way as Burns's poem on the mouse; but his later poem, "The Titmouse," has many of the same qualities, and cannot fail to be acceptable to both poet and nature alist.

The chickadee is indeed a truly Emersonian bird, and the poet shows him to be J both a hero and a philosopher. Hardy, active, social, a winter bird no less than a summer, a defier of both frost and heat, lover of the pine-tree, and diligent searcher after truth in the shape of eggs and larvæ of insects, pre-eminently a New England bird, clad in black and ashen grey, with a note the most cheering and reassuring to be heard in our January woods,—I know of none other of our birds so well calculated to captivate the Emersonian muse.

Emerson himself is a northern hyperborean genius—a winter bird with a clear, saucy, cheery call, and not a passionate summer songster. His lines have little melody to the ear, but they have the vigour and distinctness of all pure and compact things. They are like the needles of the pine—" the snow-loving pine "—more than the emotional foliage of the deciduous trees, and the titmouse becomes them well

" Up and away for life! be fleet !—
The frost-king ties my fumbling feet,
Sings in my ears, my hands are stones,
Curdles the blood to the marble bones,
Tugs at the heart-strings, numbs the sense,
And hems in life with narrowing fence.

Well, in this broad bed lie and sleep,
The punctual stars will vigil keep ;
Embalmed by purifying cold,
The wind shall sing their dead-march old;

The snow is no ignoble shroud,
The moon thy mourner, and the cloud.

Softly,—but this way fate was pointing,
'Twas coming fast to such anointing,
When piped a tiny voice hard by,
Gay and polite, a cheerful cry,
Chick-chickadeedee saucy note,
Out of sound heart and merry throat,
As if it said, ' Good day, good sir !
Fine afternoon, old passenger !
Happy to meet you in these places,
Where January brings few faces.'

This poet, though he lived apart,
Moved by his hospitable heart,
Sped, when I passed his sylvan fort,
To do the honours of his court,
As fits a feathered lord of land;
Flew near, with soft wing grazed my hand,
Hopped on the bough, then darting low,
Prints his small impress on the snow,
Shows feats of his gymnastic play,
Head downward, clinging to the spray.

Here was this atom in full breath,
Hurling defiance at vast death;
This scrap of valour just for play
Fronts the north-wind in waistcoat grey,
As if to shame my weak behaviour;
I greeted loud my little saviour,
' You pet! what dost here ? and what for ?
In these woods, thy small Labrador,

At this pinch, wee San Salvador!
What fire burns in that little chest,
So frolic, stout, and self-possest ?
Henceforth I wear no stripe but thine;
Ashes and jet all hues outshine.
Why are not diamonds black and grey ?
And I affirm the spacious north
Exists to draw thy virtue forth.
I think no virtue goes with size;
The reason of all cowardice
Is, that men are overgrown,
And to be valiant, must come down
To the titmouse dimension.'

I think old Caesar must have heard
In northern Gaul my dauntless bird,
And, echoed in some frosty wold,
Borrowed thy battle-numbers bold.
And I will write our annals new
And thank thee for a better clew.
I, who dreamed not when I came here
To find the antidote of fear,
Now hear thee say in Roman key,
Pæan I Veni, vidi, vici"

A late bird-poem and a good one of its kind is Celia Thaxter's " Sandpiper," which recalls Bryant's "Water-fowl" in its successful rendering of the spirit and at-mosphere of the scene and the distinctness with which the lone bird, flitting along the beach, is brought before the mind. It is a woman's, or a feminine, poem, as Bry-ant's is characteristically a man's.

The sentiment or feeling awakened by any of the aquatic fowls is pre-eminent-ly one of loneliness. The wood-duck which your approach starts from the pond or the marsh, the loon neighing down out of the April sky, the wild goose, the curlew, the stork, the bittern, the sandpiper, etc., awaken quite a different train of emotions from those awakened by the land-birds. They all have clinging to them some reminiscence and suggestion of the sea. Their cries echo its wildness and desolation ; their wings are the shape of its billows.

Of the sandpipers there are many varieties, found upon the coast and penetrating inland along the rivers and water-courses, the smallest of the species, commonly called the "tip-up," going up all the mountain brooks and breeding in the sand along their banks ; but the characteristics are the same in all, and the eye detects little difference except in size.

The walker on the beach sees him running or flitting before him, following up the breakers and picking up the aquatic insects left on the sands ; and the trout-fisher along the furthest inland stream likewise intrudes upon its privacy. Flitting along from stone, to stone seeking its food, the hind part of its body "teetering" up and down, its soft grey colour blending it with the pebbles and the rocks; or else skimming up or down the stream on its long convex wings, uttering its shrill cry, the sandpiper is not a bird of the sea merely; and Mrs. Thaxter's poem is as much for the dweller inland as the dweller upon the coast.

" THE SANDPIPER.

' Across the narrow beach we flit,
One little sandpiper and I; And fast I gather, bit by bit,
The scattered driftwood bleached and dry. The wild waves reach their hands for it,
The wild wind raves, the tide runs high, As up and down the beach we flit,—
One little sandpiper and I.

Above our heads the sullen clouds
Scud black and swift across the sky;
like silent ghosts in misty shrouds

Stand out the white lighthouses high.

Almost as far as eye can reach
I see the close-reefed vessels fly,
As fast we flit along the beach,—
One little sandpiper and I.

I watch him as he skims along,
Uttering his sweet and mournful cry;
He starts not at my fitful song,
Or flash of fluttering drapery;
He has no thought of any wrong;
He scans me with a fearless eye.
Staunch friends are we, well tried and strong,
The little sandpiper and I.

Comrade, where wilt thou be to-night
When the loosed storm breaks furiously ? My driftwood fire will burn so
bright!
To what warm shelter canst thou fly ? I do not fear for thee, though wroth
The tempest rushes through the sky ; For are we not God's children both,
Thou, little sandpiper, and I ?"

Others of our birds have been game for the poetic muse, but in most cases the
poets have had some moral or pretty conceit to I convey, and have not loved the
bird first. I Mr. Lathrop preaches a little in his pleasant ! poem, "The Sparrow," but
he must sometime have looked upon the bird with genuine emotion to have written
the first two stanzas

" Glimmers gay the leafless thicket ,
Close beside my garden gate,
Where, so light, from post to wicket,
Hops the sparrow, blithe, sedate;

Who, with meekly folded wing,
Comes to sun himself and sing.

It was there, perhaps, last year,
That his little house he built;
For he seems to perk and peer,
And to twitter, too, and tilt
The bare branches in between,
With a fond, familiar mien."

The bluebird has not been overlooked, and (Halleck, Longfellow, and Mrs. Sigourney have written poems upon him; but from none of them does there fall that first note of his in early spring—a note that may be called the violet of sound, and as welcome to the ear, heard above the cold damp earth, as is its floral type to the eye a few weeks later. Lowell's two lines come nearer the mark :—
" The bluebird, shifting his light load of song
From post to post along the cheerless fence."

Or the first swallow that comes twittering up the southern valley, laughing a gleeful childish laugh, and awakening such memories in the heart, who has put him in a poem ? So the humming-bird too escapes through the finest meshes of rhyme.

The most melodious of our songsters, the wood-thrush and hermit-thrush—birds whose strains, more than any others, express har-' mony and serenity—have not, as I am aware of, yet had reared to them their merited poetic monument—unless indeed the already named poet of the mocking-bird has done this service for the hermit-thrush in his " President Lincoln's Burial Hymn." Here the threnody is blent of three chords, the blossoming lilac, the evening star, and the hermit-thrush, the latter playing the most prominent part throughout the composition. It is the exalting and spiritual utterance of the " solitary singer" that calms and consoles the poet, when the powerful shock of the President's assassination comes upon him, and he flees from the stifling atmosphere and offensive lights and conversation of the house,

" Forth to hiding, receiving night that talks not,
Down to the shores of the water, the path by the swamp in the dimness,
To the solemn shadowy cedars and ghostly pines so still.

"Numerous others of our birds would seem to challenge attention by their calls and notes. There is the Maryland yellow-throat, for instance, standing in the door of his bushy tent, and calling out as you approach, *"which way, sir!" "which way, sir!"* If he says this to the ear of common folk, what would he not say to the poet ? One of the pewees says *" stay there!"* with great emphasis. The cardinal grossbeak calls out *"what cheer," "what cheer;"* the bluebird says *"purity," "purity," "purity;"* the brown-thrasher, or ferruginous thrush, according to Thoreau, calls out to the farmer planting his corn, *"drop it," "drop it,"* "cover it up," " cover it up." The yellow breasted chat says *"who," "who,"* and *"tea-boy."* What the robin says, carolling that simple strain from the top of the tall maple, or the crow with his hardy *haw-haw,* or the pedestrian meadow-lark sounding his piercing and long-drawn note in the spring meadows, the poets ought to be able to tell us. I only know the birds all have a language which is very expressive, and which is easily translatable into the human tongue.

TOUCHES OF NATURE.
I

WHEREVER Nature has commissioned one creature to prey upon another, she has preserved the balance by forewarning that other creature of what she has done. Nature says to the cat, " Catch the mouse," and she equips her for that purpose ; but on the selfsame day she says to the mouse, " Be wary—the cat is watching for you." Nature takes care that none of her creatures have smooth sailing, the whole voyage at least. Why has she not made the musquito noiseless and its bite itchless? Simply because in that case the odds would be too greatly in its favour. She has taken especial pains to enable the owl to fly softly and silently, because the creatures it preys upon are small and wary, and never venture far from their holes. She has not shown the same caution in the case of the crow, because the crow feeds on dead flesh or on grubs and beetles, or fruit and grain, that do not need to be approached stealthily. The big fish love to eat up the little fish, and the little fish know it, and on the very day they are hatched seek shallow water, and put little sand bars between themselves and their too loving parents.

How easily a bird's tail, or that of any fowl, or in fact any part of the plumage, comes out when the hold of its would-be capturer is upon this alone; and how hard it yields in the dead bird. No doubt there is relaxation in the former case. Nature says to the pursuer, "Hold on," and to the pursued, "Let your tail go." What is the tortuous zigzag course of those slow-flying moths for but to make it difficult for the birds to snap them up? The skunk is a slow, witless creature, and the fox and lynx love its meat; yet it carries a bloodless weapon that neither likes to face.

I recently heard of an ingenious method a certain other simple and slow-going creature has of baffling its enemy. A friend of mine was walking in the fields when he saw a commotion in the grass a few yards off. Approaching the spot, he found a snake— the common garter snake—trying to swallow a lizard. And how do you suppose the lizard was defeating the benevolent designs of the snake ? By simply taking hold of its own tail and making itself into a hoop. The snake went round and round and could find neither beginning nor end. Who was the old giant that found himself wrestling with Time ? This little snake had a tougher customer the other day in the bit of eternity it was trying to swallow.

The snake itself has not the same wit, because I lately saw a black snake in the woods trying to swallow the garter snake, and he had made some headway, though the little snake was fighting every inch of the ground, hooking his tail about sticks and bushes, and pulling back with all his might, apparently not liking the look of things down there at all. I thought it well to let him have a good taste of his own doctrines, when I put my foot down against further proceedings.

This arming of one creature against another is often cited as an evidence of the wisdom of Nature, but it is rather an evidence of her impartiality. She does not care a fig more for one creature than for another, and is equally on the side of both, or perhaps it would be better to say she does not care a fig for either. Every creature must take its chances, and man is no exception. We can ride if we know how and are going her way, or we can be run over if we fall or make a mistake. Nature does not care whether the hunter slay the beast or the beast the hunter; she will make good compost of them both, and her ends are prospered whichever succeed.

"If the red slayer thinks he slays,
Or if the slain think he is slain,
They know not well the subtle ways
I keep, and pass, and turn again."

What is the end of Nature? Where is the end of a sphere ? The sphere balances at any and every point. So everything in Nature is at the top, and yet no one thing is at the top.

She works with reference to no measure of time, no limit of space, and with an abundance of material not expressed by exhaustless. Did you think Niagara a great exhibition of power? What is that, then, that withdraws noiseless and invisible in the ground about,,and of which Niagara is but the lifting of the finger ?

Nature is thoroughly selfish, and looks only to her own ends. One thing she is bent upon, and that is keeping up the supply, multiplying endlessly and scattering as she multiplies. Did Nature have in view our delectation when she made the apple, the peach, the plum, the cherry, etc. ? Undoubtedly ; but only as a means to her own private ends. What a bribe or a wage is the pulp of these delicacies to all creatures to come and sow their seed! And Nature has taken care to make the seed indigestible, so that though the fruit be eaten, the germ is not, but only planted.

God made the crab, but man made the pippin; but the pippin cannot propagate itself, and exists only by violence and usurpation. Bacon says, "It is easier to deceive Nature than to force her," but it seems to me the nurserymen really force her. They cut off the head of a savage and clap on the head of a fine gentleman, and the crab becomes a Swaar or a Baldwin. Or is it a kind of deception practised upon Nature, which succeeds only by being carefully concealed ? If we could play the same tricks upon her in the human species, how the great geniuses could be preserved and propagated, and the world stocked with them. But what a frightful condition of things that would be! No new men, but a tiresome and endless repetition of the old ones—a world perpetually stocked with Newtons and Shakespeares.

We say 'Nature knows best, and has adapted this or that to our wants or to our constitution—sound to the ear, light and colour to the eye, etc.; but she has not done any such thing, but has adapted man to these things. The physical cosmos is the mould, and man is the molten metal that is poured into it. The light fashioned the eye, the laws of sound made the ear; in fact man is the outcome of Nature and not the reverse. Creatures that live for ever in the dark have no eyes; and would not any one of our senses perish and be shed, as it were, in a world where it could not be used ?

II

It is well to let down our metropolitan pride a little. Man thinks himself at the top, and that the immense display and prodigality of Nature are for him. But they are no more for him than they are for the birds and beasts, and he is no more at the top than they are. He appeared upon the stage when the play had advanced to a certain point, and he will disappear from the stage when the play has reached another point, and the great drama go on without him. The geological ages, the convulsions and parturition throes of the globe, were to bring him forth no more than the beetles. Is not all this wealth of the seasons, these solar and sidereal influences, this depth and vitality and internal fire, these seas, and rivers, and oceans, and atmospheric currents, as necessary to the life of the ants and worms we tread under foot as to our own ? And does the sun shine for me any more than for yon butterfly ? What I mean to say is, we cannot put our finger upon this or that, and say here is the end of Nature. The Infinite cannot be measured. The plan of Nature is so immense—but she has no plan, no scheme, but to go on and on for ever. What is size, what is time, distance, etc., to the Infinite? Nothing. The Infinite knows no time, no space, no great, no small, no beginning, no end.

I sometimes think that the earth and the worlds are a kind of nervous ganglia in an organisation of which we can form no conception, or less even than that. If one of the globules of blood that circulate in our veins was magnified enough million times, we might see a globe teeming with life and power. Such is this earth of ours, coursing in the veins of the Infinite. Size is only relative, and the imagination finds no end to the series either way.

III

Looking out of the car window one day, I saw the pretty and unusual sight of an eagle sitting upon the ice in the river, surrounded by half a dozen or more crows. The crows appeared as if looking up to the noble bird and attending his movements. " Are those its young ? " asked a gentleman by my side. How much did that man know—not about eagles, but about Nature? If he had been familiar with geese or hens, or with donkeys, he would not have asked that question. The ancients had an axiom that he who knew one truth knew all truths; so much else becomes knowable when one vital fact is thoroughly known. You have a key, a standard, and cannot be deceived. Chemistry, geology, astronomy, natural history, all admit one to the same measureless interiors.

I heard a great man say that he could see how much of the theology of the day would fall before the standard of him who had got even the insects. And let any one set about studying these creatures carefully, and he will see the force of the remark. We learn the tremendous doctrine of metamorphosis from the insect world; and have not the bee and the ant taught man wisdom from the first ? I was highly edified the past summer by observing the ways and doings of a colony of black hornets that established themselves under one of the projecting gables of my house. This hornet has the reputation of being a very ugly customer, but I found it no trouble to live on the most friendly terms with them. They were as little disposed to quarrel as I was. It is indeed the eagle among hornets, and very noble and dignified in its bear-ing. They used to come freely into the house and prey upon the flies. You would hear that deep, mellow hum, and see the black falcon poising on wing, or striking here and there at the flies, that scattered on his approach like chickens before a hawk. When he had caught one he would alight upon some object and proceed to dress and draw his game. The wings were sheared off, the legs cut away, the bristles trimmed, then the body thoroughly bruised and broken. When the work was completed, the fly was rolled up into a small pellet, and with it under his arm the hornet flew to his nest, where, no doubt, in due time it was properly served up on the royal board. Every dinner inside these paper walls is a state dinner, for the queen bee is always present.

I used to mount the ladder to within two or three feet of the nest and observe the proceedings. I at first thought the workshop must be inside—a place where the pulp was mixed and perhaps treated with chemicals ; for each bee when he came with his burden of materials passed into the nest, and then, after a few moments, emerged again and crawled to the place of building. But I one day stopped up the entrance with some cotton, when no one happened to be on guard, and then observed that when the loaded bee could not get inside, he, after some deliberation, proceeded to the unfinished part and went forward with his work. Hence I inferred that may be the bee went inside to report and to receive orders, or possibly to surrender its material into fresh hands. Its career when away from the nest is beset with dangers; the colony is never large, and the safe return of every bee is no doubt a matter of solicitude to the royal mother.

The hornet was the first paper-maker, and holds the original patent. The paper it makes is about like that of the newspaper; nearly as firm, and made of essentially the same material—woody fibres scraped from old rails and boards. And there is news on it too, if one could make out the characters.

When I stopped the entrance with cotton there was no commotion or excitement, as there would have been in the case of yellow-jackets. Those outside went to pulling, and those inside went to pushing and chewing. Only once did one of the outsiders come down and look me suspiciously in the face, and inquire very plainly what my business might be up there. I bowed my head, being at the top of a twenty-foot ladder, and had nothing to say.

The cotton was chewed and moistened about the edges till every fibre was loosened, when the mass dropped. But instantly the entrance was made smaller, and changed so as to make the feat of stopping it more difficult.

IV.

There are those who look at Nature from the standpoint of conventional and artificial life—from parlour windows and through gilt-edged poems—the sentimentalists. At the other extreme are those who do not look at Nature at all, but are a grown part of her, and look away from her toward the other class—the backwoodsmen and pioneers, and all rude and simple persons. Then there are those in whom the two are united or merged—the great poets and artists. In them the sentimentalist is corrected and cured, and the hairy and taciturn frontiersman has had experience to some purpose. The true poet knows more about Nature than the naturalist because he carries her open secrets in his heart. Eckerman could instruct Goethe in ornithology, but could not Goethe instruct Eckerman in the meaning and mystery of the bird? It is my privilege to number among my friends a man who has passed his life in cities amid the throngs of men, who never goes to the woods or to the country, or hunts or fishes, and yet he is the true naturalist. I think he studies the orbs. I think day and night and the stars and the faces of men and women have taught him all there is worth knowing.

We run to Nature because we are afraid of man. Our artists paint the landscape because they cannot paint the human face. If we could look into the eyes of a man as coolly as we can into the eyes of an animal, the products of our pens and brushes would be quite different from what they are

V.

But I suspect after all it makes but little difference to which school you go, whether to the woods or to the city. A sincere man learns pretty much the same things in both places. The differences are superficial, the resemblances deep and many. The hermit is a hermit and the poet a poet, whether he grow up in the town or the country. I was forcibly reminded of this fact recently on opening the works of Charles Lamb after I had been reading those of our Henry Thoreau. Lamb cared nothing for Nature, Thoreau for little else. One was as attached to the city and the life of the street and tavern as the other to the country and the life of animals and plants. Yet they are close akin. They give out the same tone and are pitched in about the same key. Their methods are the same; so are .their quaintness and scorn of rhetoric. Thoreau has the drier humour, as might be expected, and is less stomachic. There is more juice and unction in Lamb, but this he owes to his nationality. Both are essayists who in a less reflective age would have been poets pure and simple. Both were spare, high-nosed men, and I fancy a resemblance even in their portraits. Thoreau is the Lamb of New England fields and woods,* and Lamb is the Thoreau of London streets and clubs. There was a wilfulness and perversity about Thoreau behind which he concealed his shyness and his thin skin, and there was a similar foil in Lamb, though less marked, on account of his good-nature; that was a part of his armour too.

VI.

Speaking of Thoreau's dry humour reminds me how surely the old English unctuous and sympathetic humour is dying out or has died out of our literature. Our first notable crop of authors had it Paulding, Cooper, Irving, and in a measure Hawthorne—but our later humorists have it not at all, but in its stead an intellectual quickness and perception of the ludicrous that is not unmixed with scorn.

One of the marks of the great humorist, like Cervantes, or Sterne, or Scott, is that he approaches his subject, not through his head merely, but through his heart, his love, his humanity. His humour is full of compassion, full of the milk of human kindness, and does not separate him from his subject, but unites him to it by vital ties. How Sterne loved Uncle Toby and sympathised with him, and Cervantes his luckless knight! I fear our humorists would have made fun of them, would have shown them up and . stood aloof superior, and " laughed a laugh of merry scorn." Whatever else the great humorist or poet, or any artist, may be or do, there is no contempt in his laughter. And this point cannot be too strongly insisted on in view of the fact that nearly all our humorous writers seem impressed with the conviction that their own dignity and self-respect require them to **look down** upon what they portray. But it is only little men who look down upon anything or speak down to anybody.

One Bees every day how clear it is that specially fine, delicate, intellectual persons cannot portray satisfactorily coarse, common, uncultured characters. Their attitude is at once scornful and supercilious. The great man, like Socrates, or Dr. Johnson, or Abraham Lincoln, is just as surely coarse as he is fine, but the complaint I make with our humorists is that they are fine and not coarse in any healthful and manly sense. A great part of the best literature and the best art is of the vital fluids, the bowels, the chest, the appetites, and is to be read and judged only through love and compassion. Let us pray for unction, which is the marrowfat of humour, and for humility, which is the badge of manhood.

As the voice of the American has retreated from his chest to his throat and nasal passages, so there is danger that his contribution to literature will soon cease to imply any blood or viscera, or healthful carnality, or depth of human and manly affection, and be the fruit entirely of our toploftical brilliancy and cleverness.

"What I complain of is just as true of the essayists and the critics as of the novelists. The prevailing tone here also is born of a feeling of immense superiority. How our lofty young men, for instance, look down upon Carlyle, and administer their masterly rebukes to him. But see how Carlyle treats Burns, or Scott, or Johnson, or Novalis, or any of his heroes. Ay, there 's the rub; he makes heroes of them. which is not a trick of small natures. He can say of Johnson that he was "moonstruck," but it is from no lofty height of fancied superiority, but he uses the word as a naturalist uses a term to describe an object he loves.

What we want, and perhaps have got more of than I am ready to admit, is a race of writers who affiliate with their subjects and enter into them through their blood, their sexuality, and manliness, instead of standing apart and criticising them and writing about them through mere intellectual cleverness and "smartness."

VII.

There is a feeling in heroic poetry or in a burst of eloquence that I sometimes catch in quite different fields. I caught it this morning, for instance, when I saw the belated trains go by, and knew how they ' had been battling with storm, darkness, and distance, and had triumphed. They were due at my place in the night, but did not pass till after eight o'clock in the morning. Two trains coupled together—the fast mail and the express—making an immense line of coaches hauled by two engines. They had come from the West, were all covered with snow and ice, like soldiers with the dust of battle upon them. They had masted their forces, and were now moving with augmented speed, and with a resolution that was epic and grand. Talk about the railroad dispelling the romance from the landscape; if it does, it brings the heroic element in. The moving train is a proud spectacle, especially in stormy and tempestuous nights. When I look out and see its light, steady and un-flickering as the planets, and hear the roar of its advancing tread, or its sound diminishing in the distance, am I comforted and made stout of heart. O night, where is thy stay! O space, where is thy victory! Or to see the fast mail pass in the morning is as good as a page of Homer. It quickens one's pulse for all day. It is the Ajax of trains. I hear its defiant, warning whistle, hear it thunder over the bridges, and its sharp, rushing ring among the rocks, and in the winter mornings see its glancing, meteoric lights, or in summer its white form bursting through the silence and the shadows, its plume of smoke lying flat upon its roofs and stretching far behind—a sight better than a battle. It is something of the same feeling one has in witnessing any wild, free careering in storms and in floods in nature, or in beholding the charge of an army, or in listening to an eloquent man, or to a hundred instruments of music in full blast—it is triumph, victory. What is eloquence but mass in motion a flood, a cataract, an express train, a cavalry charge? We are literally carried away, swept from our feet, and recover our senses again as best we can.

I experienced the same emotion when I saw them go by with the sunken steamer. The procession moved slowly and solemnly. It was like a funeral cortege,—a long line of grim floats and barges and boxes, with their bowed and solemn derricks—the pall-bearers and underneath in her watery grave, where she had been for six months, the sunken steamer, partially lifted and borne along. Next day the procession went back again, and the spectacle was still more eloquent. The steamer had been taken to the flats above, and raised till her walking beam was out of water; her bell also was exposed and cleaned and rung, and the wreckers' Herculean labour seemed nearly over. But that night the winds and the storms held high carnival. It looked like preconcerted action on the part of tide, tempest, and rain, to defeat these wreckers, for the elements all pulled together and pulled till cables and hawser snapped like threads. Back the procession started, anchors were dragged or lost, immense new cables were quickly taken ashore and fastened to trees; but no use, trees were upturned, the cables stretched till they grew small and sang like harp strings, then parted; back, back against the desperate efforts of the men, till within a few feet of her old grave, when there was a great commotion among the craft, floats were overturned, enormous chains parted, colossal timbers were snapped like pipestems, and with a sound that filled all the air, the steamer plunged to the bottom again in seventy feet of water.

VIII.

I am glad to observe that all the poetry of the midsummer harvesting has not gone out with the scythe and the whetstone. The line of mowers was a pretty sight, if one did not sympathise too deeply with the human backs turned up there to the sun, and the sound of the whetstone, coming up from the meadows in the dewy morning, was pleasant music. But I find the sound of the mowing-machine and the patent reaper are even more in tune with the voices of nature at this season. The characteristic sounds of midsummer are the sharp, whirring crescendo of the cicada or harvest fly, and the rasping, stridulous notes of the nocturnal insects. The mowing-machine repeats and imitates these sounds. 'Tis like the hum of a locust or the shuffling of a mighty grasshopper. More than that, the grass and the grain at this season have become hard. The timothy stalk is like a flie; the rye straw is glazed with flint; the grasshoppers snap sharply as they fly up in front of you, the bird-songs have ceased, the ground crackles under foot, the eye of day is brassy and merciless, and in harmony with all these things is the rattle of the mower and hay tedder.

IX.

'Tis an evidence of how directly we are related to Nature, that we more or less sympathise with the weather, and take on the colour of the day. Goethe said he worked easiest on a high barometer. One is like a chimney that draws well some days and won't draw at all on others, and the secret is mainly in the condition of the atmosphere. Anything positive and decided with the weather is a good omen. A pouring rain may be more auspicious than a sleeping sunshine. When the stove draws well the fogs and fumes will leave your mind.

I find there is great virtue in the bare ground, and have been much put out at times by those white angelic days we have in winter, such as Whittier has so well described in these lines :—

"Around the glistening wonder bent
The blue walls of the firmament;
No cloud above, no earth below,
A universe of sky and snow."

On such days my spirit gets snow blind ; all things take on the same colour, or no colour; my thought loses its perspective; the inner world is a blank like the outer, and all my great ideals are wrapped in the same monotonous and expressionless commonplace. The blackest of black days are better.

Why does snow so kill the landscape and blot out our interest in it ? Not merely because it is cold, and the symbol of death, for I imagine as many inches of apple blossoms would have about the same effect; but because it expresses nothing. White is a negative; a perfect blank. The eye was made for colour, and for the earthy tints, and when these are denied it, the mind is very apt to sympathise and to suffer also.

Then when the sap begins to mount in the trees, and the spring languor comes, does not one grow restless indoors? The sun puts out the fire, the people say, and the spring sun certainly makes one's intellectual light grow dim. Why should not a man sympathise with the seasons and the moods and phases of Nature? He is an apple upon ·this tree, or rather he is a babe at this breast, and what his great mother feels affects him also.

X.

I have frequently been surprised, in late fall and early winter, to see how unequal or irregular was the encroachment of the frost upon the earth. If there is suddenly a great fall in the mercury, the frost lays siege to the soil and effects a lodgment here and there, and extends its conquests gradually. At one place in the field you can easily run your staff through into the soft ground, when a few rods further on it will be as hard as a rock. A little covering of dry grass or leaves is a great protection. The moist places hold out long, and the spring runs never freeze. You find the frost has gone several inches into the ploughed ground, but on going to the woods and poking away the leaves and débris under the hemlocks and cedars, you find there is no frost at all. The earth freezes her ears, and toes. and naked places first, and her body last.

If heat was visible, or if we represent it say by smoke, then the December landscape would present a curious spectacle. We would see the smoke lying low over the meadows, thickest in the hollows and moist places, and where the turf was oldest and densest. It would cling to the fences and ravines. Under every evergreen tree we would see the vapour rising and filling the branches, while the woods of pine and hemlock would be blue with it long after it had disappeared from the open country. It would rise from the tops of the trees and be carried this way and that with the wind. The valleys of the great rivers, like the Hudson, would overflow with it Large bodies of water become regular magazines in which heat is stored during the summer, and they give it out again during the fall and early winter. The early frosts keep well back from the Hudson, skulking behind the ridges, and hardly come over in sight at any point. But they grow bold as the season advances, till the river's fires too are put out, and winter covers it with his snows.

One of the strong and original strokes of Nature was when she made the loon. It is always refreshing to contemplate a creature so positive and characteristic. He is the great diver and flier under water. The loon is the genus loci of the wild northern lakes, as solitary as they are. Some birds represent the majesty of Nature, like the eagles ; others its ferocity, like the hawks; others its cunning, like the crow; others its sweetness and melody, like the song-birds. The loon represents its wildness and solitariness. It is cousin to the beaver. It has the feathers of a bird and the fur of an animal, and the heart of both. It is as quick and cunning as it is bold and resolute. It dives with such marvellous quickness that the shot of the gunner get there just in time "to cut across a circle of descending tail feathers and a couple of little jets of water flung upward by the web feet of the loon." When disabled so that it can neither dive nor fly, it is said to face its foe, look him in the face with its clear, piercing eye, and fight resolutely till death. The gunners say there is something in its wailing, piteous cry, when dying, almost human in its agony. The loon is, in the strictest sense, an aquatic fowl. It can barely walk upon the land, and one species at least cannot take flight from the shore. But in the water its feet are more than feet, and its wings more than wings. It plunges into this denser air, and flies with incredible speed. Its head and beak form a sharp point to its tapering neck. Its wings are far in front, and its legs equally far in the rear, and its course through the crystal depths is like the speed of an arrow. In the northern lakes it has been taken forty feet under water upon hooks baited for the great lake trout. I had never seen one till last fall, when one appeared on the river in front of my house. I knew instantly it was the loon. Who could not tell a loon a half-mile or more away, though he had never seen one before ? The river was like glass, and every movement of the bird as it sported about broke the surface into ripples, that revealed it far and wide. Presently a boat shot out from shore, and went ripping up the surface toward the loon. The creature at once seemed to divine the intentions of the boatman, and sidled off obliquely, keeping a sharp lookout as if to make sure it was pursued. A steamer came down and passed between them, and when the way was again clear the loon was still swimming on the surface. Presently it disappeared under the water, and the boatman pulled sharp and hard. In a few moments the bird reappeared some rods further on, as if to make an observation. Seeing it was being pursued, and no mistake, it dived quickly, and when it came up again, had gone many times as far as the boat had in the same space of time. Then it dived again, and distanced its pursuer so easily that he gave over the chase and rested upon his oars. But the bird made a final plunge, and when it emerged upon the surface again it was over one mile away. Its course must have been, and doubtless was, an actual flight under water, and half as fast as the crow flies in the air.

The loon would have delighted the old poets. Its wild, demoniac laughter awakens the echoes on the solitary lakes, and its ferity and hardiness was kindred to those robust spirits.

XII.

One notable difference between man and the four-footed animals which has often occurred to me is in the eye, and the greater perfection, or rather supremacy of the sense of sight in the human species. All the animals—the dog, the fox, wolf, deer, cow, horse, etc. depend mainly upon the senses of hearing and smell. Almost their entire powers of discrimination are confined to these two senses. The dog picks his master out of the crowd by smell, and the cow her calf out of the herd. Sight is only partial recognition. The question can only be settled beyond all doubt by the aid of the nose. The fox, alert and cunning as he is, will pass within a few yards of the hunter, and not know him from a stump. A squirrel will run across your lap, and a marmot between your feet if you are motionless. When a herd of cattle see a strange object they are not satisfied till each one has sniffed it; and the horse is cured of his fright at the robe, or the meal-bag, or other object, as soon as he can be induced to smell it. There is a great deal of speculation in the eye of an animal, but very little science. Then you cannot catch an animal's eye; he looks at you, but not into your eye. The dog directs his gaze toward your face, but for aught you can tell it centres upon your mouth or nose. The same with your horse or cow. Their eye is vague and indefinite.

Not so with the birds. The bird has the human eye in its clearness, its power, and its supremacy over the other senses. How acute their sense of smell may be is uncertain; their hearing is sharp enough, but their vision is the most remarkable. A crow or a hawk, or any of the larger birds, will not mistake you for a stump, or rock, stand you never so still amid the bushes. But they cannot separate you from your horse or team. A hawk reads a man on horseback as one animal, and reads it as a horse. None of the sharp-scented animals could be thus deceived.

The bird has man's brain also in its size. The brain of a song-bird is even much larger in proportion than that of the greatest human monarch, and its life is correspondingly intense and high-strung. But the bird's eye is superficial. It is on the outside of his head. It is round that it may take in a full circle at a glance.

All the quadrupeds emphasise their direct forward gaze by a corresponding movement of the ears, as if to supplement and aid one sense with another. But man's eye seldom needs the confirmation of his ear, while it is so set, and his head so poised, that his look is forcible and pointed without being thus seconded.

XIII.

I once saw a cow that had lost her end. Show forlorn and desolate and sick at heart that cow looked ! No more rumination, no J more of that second and finer mastication, (no more of that sweet and juicy reverie under the spreading trees, or in the stall. Then the farmer took an elder and scraped the bark, and put something with it, and made the cow a cud, and after due waiting the experiment took, a response came back, and the mysterious machinery was once more inmotion, and the cow was herself again.

Have you, O poet, or essayist, or story writer, never lost your cud and wandered about days and weeks without being able to start a single thought or an image that tasted good—your literary appetite dull or all gone, and the conviction daily growing that it is all over with you in that direction? A little elder bark, something fresh and bitter from the woods, is about the best thing you can take.

XIV.

Notwithstanding what I have elsewhere said about the desolation of snow, when one looks closely it is little more than a thin veil after all, and takes and repeats the form of whatever it covers. Every path through the fields is just as plain as before. On every hand the ground sends tokens, and the curves and slopes are not of the snow, but of the earth beneath. In like.manner the rankest vegetation hides the ground less than we think. Looking across a wide valley in the month of July, I have noted that the fields, except the meadows, had a ruddy tinge, and that corn which near at hand seemed to completely envelop the soil, at that distance gave only a slight shade of green. The colour of the ground everywhere predominated, and I doubt not if we could see the earth from a point sufficiently removed, as from the moon, its ruddy hue, like that of Mars, would alone be visible.

What is a man but a miniature earth, with many disguises in the way of manners, possessions, dissemblances, etc.? Yet through all—through all the work of his hands and all the thoughts of his mind—how surely the ground quality of him, the fundamental hue, whether it be this or that, makes itself felt, and is alone important.

Men follow their noses, it is said. I have wondered why the Greek did not follow his nose in architecture—did not copy those arches that spring from it as from a pier, and support his brow—but always and everywhere used the post and the lintel. There was something in that face that has never reappeared in the human countenance. I am thinking especially of that straight, strong profile. Is it really godlike, or is this impression the result of association? But any suggestion or reminiscence of it in the modern face at once gives one the idea of strength. It is a face strong in the loins, or it suggests a high, elastic instep. It is the face of order and proportion. Those arches are the symbols of law and self-control. The point of greatest interest is the union of the nose with the brow,—that strong high embankment; it makes the bridge from the ideal to the real sure and easy. All his ideas passed readily into form. In the modern face the arches are more or less crushed, and the nose severed from the brow —hence the abstract and the analytic; hence the preponderance of the speculative intellect over creative power.

XVI.

I have thought that the boy is the only true lover of Nature, and that we who make such a dead set at studying and admiring her come very wide of the mark. "The nonchalance of a boy who is sure of his dinner," says our Emerson, "is the healthy attitude of humanity." The boy is a part of Nature; he is as indifferent, as careless, as vagrant as she. He browses, he digs, he hunts, he climbs, he hallooes, he feeds on roots, and greens, and mast. He uses things roughly and without sentiment. The coolness with which boys will drown dogs or cats, or hang them to trees, or murder young birds, or torture frogs or squirrels, is like Nature's own mercilessness.

Certain it is that we often get some of the best touches of nature from children. Childhood is a world by itself, and we listen to children when they frankly speak out of it with a strange interest. There is such a freedom from responsibility and from worldly wisdom—it is heavenly wisdom. There is no sentiment in children, because there is no ruin; nothing has gone to decay about them yet—not a leaf or twig. Until he is well into his teens, and sometimes later, a boy is like a bean-pod before the fruit has developed—indefinite, succulent, rich in possibilities which are only vaguely outlined. He is a pericarp merely. How rudimental are all his ideas. I knew a boy who began his school composition on swallows by saying there were two kinds of swallows —chimney swallows and swallows.

Girls come to themselves sooner; are indeed from the first more definite and "translatable."

XVII.

Who will write the natural history of the boy? One of the first points to be taken account of is his clannishness. The boys of one neighbourhood are always pitted against those of an adjoining neighbourhood, or of one end of the town against those of the other end. A bridge, a river, a railroad track, are always boundaries of hostile or semi-hostile tribes. The boys that go up the road from the country school hoot derisively at those that go down the road, and not infrequently add the insult of stones; and the down-roaders return the hooting and the missiles with interest.

Often there is open war, and the boys meet and have regular battles. A few years since the boys of two rival towns on opposite sides of the Ohio river became so belligerent that the authorities had to interfere. Whenever an Ohio boy was caught on the West Virginia side of the river he was unmercifully beaten, and when a West Virginia boy was discovered on the Ohio side, he was pounced upon in the same manner. One day a vast number of boys, about one hundred and fifty on a side, met by appointment upon the ice and engaged in a pitched battle. Every conceivable missile was used, including pistols. The battle, says the local paper, raged with fury for about two hours. One boy received a wound behind the ear, from the effects of which he died the next morning. More recently the boys of a large manufacturing town of New Jersey were divided into two hostile clans that came into frequent collision. One Saturday both Bides mustered its forces, and a regular fight ensued, one boy here also losing his life from the encounter.

Every village and settlement is at times the scene of these youthful collisions. When a new boy appears in the village, or at the ' country school, how the other boys crowd around him and take his measure, or pick at him and insult him to try his mettle. –

I knew a boy, twelve or thirteen years old, who was sent to help a drover with some cattle as far as a certain village ten miles from his home. After the place was reached, and while the boy was eating his cracker and candies, he strolled about the village, and fell in with some other boys playing upon a bridge. In a short time a large number of children of all sizes had collected upon the bridge. The new-comer was presently challenged by the boys of his own age to jump with them. This he readily did, and cleared their farthest mark. Then he gave them a sample of his

stone-throwing, and at this pastime he also far surpassed his competitors. Before long the feeling of the crowd began to set against him, showing itself first in the smaller fry, who began half playfully to throw pebbles and lumps of dry earth at him. Then they would run up slyly and strike him with sticks. Presently the large ones began to tease him in like manner, till the contagion of hostility spread, and the whole pack was arrayed against the strange boy. He kept them at bay for a few moments with his stick, till, the feeling mounting higher and higher, he broke through their ranks, and fled precipitately toward home, with the throng of little and big at his heels. Gradually the
girls and smaller boys dropped behind, till at the end of the first fifty rods only two boys of about his own size, with wrath and determination in their faces, kept up the pursuit. But to these he added the final insult of beating them at running also, and reached, much blown, a point beyond which they refused to follow.

The world the boy lives in is separate and distinct from the world the man lives in. It is a world inhabited only by boys. No events are important or of any moment save those affecting boys. How they ignore the presence of their elders' on the street, shouting out their invitations, their appointments, their pass-words from our midst, as from the veriest solitude. They have peculiar calls, whistles, signals, by which they communicate with each other at long distances like birds or wild creatures. And there is as genuine a wildness about these notes and calls as about those of a fox or coon.

The boy is a savage, a barbarian, in his taste—devouring roots, leaves, bark, unripe fruit, etc.; and in the kind of music or discord he delights in,—of harmony he has no perception. He has his fashions that spread from city to city. In one of our large cities the rage at one time was an old tin can with a string attached, out of which they tortured the most savage and ear-splitting discords. The police was obliged to interfere and suppress the nuisance. On another occasion, at Christmas, they all came forth with tin horns, and nearly drove the town distracted with the hideous uproar.

Another savage trait of the boy is his untruthfulness. Corner him, and the chances are ten to one he will lie his way out. Conscience is a plant of slow growth in the boy. If caught in one lie, he invents another. I knew a boy who was in the habit of eating apples in school. His teacher finally caught him in the act, and without removing his eye from him, called him to' the middle of the floor.

"I saw you this time," said the teacher.
" Saw me what ?" said the boy innocently.
" Bite that apple," replied the teacher.
" No, sir," said the rascal.
" Open your mouth ; " and from its depths the teacher, with his thumb and finger, took out the piece of apple.
" Didn't know it was there," said the boy, unabashed.
Nearly all the moral sentiment and graces are late in maturing in the boy. He has no proper self-respect till past his majority. Of course there are exceptions, but they are mostly windfalls. The good boys die young. We lament the wickedness and thoughtlessness of the young vagabonds at the same time that we know it is mainly the acridity and bitterness of the unripe fruit that we are lamenting.

A BIRD MEDLEY.

PEOPLE who have not made friends with the birds do not know how much they miss. Especially to one living in the country, of strong local attachments, and an observing turn of mind, does an acquaintance with the birds form a close and invaluable tie. The only time I saw Thomas Carlyle, I remember his relating, àpropos of this subject, that in his earlier days he was sent on a journey to a distant town on some business that gave him much bother and vexation, and that on his way back home, forlorn and dejected, he suddenly heard the larks singing all about him— soaring and singing, just as they did about his father's fields, and it had the effect to comfort him and cheer him up amazingly.

Most lovers of the birds can doubtless recall similar experiences from their own lives. Nothing wonts me to a new place more than the birds. I go, for instance, to take up my abode in the country,—to plant myself upon unfamiliar ground. I know nobody, and nobody knows me. The roads, the fields, the hills, the streams, the woods are all strange. I look wistfully upon them, but they know me not. They give back nothing to my yearning gaze. But there, on every hand, are the long-familiar birds—the same ones I left behind me, the same ones I knew in my, youth—robins, sparrows, swallows, bobolinks, crows, hawks, high-holes, meadow-larks, etc., all there before me, and ready to renew and perpetuate the old associations. Before my house is begun theirs is completed ; before I have taken root at all they are thoroughly established. I do not yet know what kind of apples my apple-trees bear, but there, in the cavity of a decayed limb, the bluebirds are building a nest, and yonder, on that branch, the social sparrow is busy with hairs and straws. The robins have tasted the quality of my cherries, and the cedar-birds have known every red cedar on the place these many years. While my house is yet surrounded by its scaffoldings, the phoebe-bird has built her exquisite mossy nest on a projecting stone beneath the eaves, a robin has filled a niche in the wall with mud and dry grass, the chimney-swallows are going out and in the chimney, and a pair of house-wrens are at home in a snug cavity over the door, and, during an April snowstorm, a number of hermit-thrushes . have taken shelter in my unfinished chambers. Indeed, I am in the midst of friends before I fairly know it. The place is not so new as I had thought. It is already old ; the birds have supplied the memories of many decades of years.

There is something almost pathetic in the fact that the birds remain for ever the same. You grow old, your friends die or move to distant lands, events sweep on and all things are changed. Yet there in your garden or orchard are the birds of your boyhood, the same notes, the same calls, and, to all intents and purposes, the identical birds endowed with perennial youth. The swallows, that built so far out of your reach beneath the eaves of your father's barn, the same ones now speak and chatter beneath the eaves of your barn. The warblers and shy wood-birds you pursued with such glee ever so many summers ago, and whose names you taught to some beloved youth who now, perchance, sleeps amid his native hills, no marks of time or change cling to them ; and when you walk out to the strange woods, there they are, mocking you with their ever-renewed and joyous youth. (The call of the high-holes, the whistle of the quail, the strong piercing note of the meadow-lark, the drumming of the grouse,—how these sounds ignore the years, and strike on the ear with the melody of that spring-time when the world was young, and life was all holiday and romance !

During any unusual tension of the feelings or emotions, how the note or song of a single bird will sink into the memory, and become inseparably associated with your grief or joy ! Shall I ever again be able to hear the song of the oriole without being pierced through and through ? Can it ever be other than a dirge for the dead to me ? Day after day, and week after week, this bird whistled and warbled in a mulberry by the door, while sorrow, like a pall, darkened my day. So loud and persistent was the singer that his note teased and worried my excited ear.

" Hearken to yon pine warbler,
Singing aloft in the tree !
Hearest thou, O traveller !
What he singeth to me ?

Not unless God made sharp thine ear
With sorrow such as mine,
Out of that delicate lay couldst thou
Its heavy tale divine."

It is the opinion of some naturalists that birds never die what is called a natural death, but come to their end by some murderous or accidental means yet I have found sparrows and vireos in the fields and woods dead or dying, that bore no marks of violence; and I remember that once in my childhood a red-bird fell down in the yard exhausted and was brought in by the girl; its bright scarlet image is indelibly stamped upon my recollection. It is not known that birds have any distempers like the domestic fowls, but I saw a social sparrow one day quite disabled by some curious malady, that suggested a disease that sometimes attacks poultry; one eye was nearly put out by a scrofulous looking sore, and on the last joint of one wing there was a large tumorous or fungous growth that crippled the bird completely. On another occasion I picked up one that appeared well but could not keep its centre of gravity when in flight, and so fell to the ground,

One reason why dead birds and animals are so rarely found is, that on the approach of death their instinct promts them to creep away in some hole or under some cover, where they would be least liable to fall a prey to their would be least to fall a prey to their natural enemies. It is doubtFul if any of the game birds, like the pigeon and grouse, ever die of old age, or. the semi-game birds like the bobolink, or the " century living " crow ; but in what other form can death overtake the humming-bird, or even the swift and the barn-swallow? Such are true birds of the air; they may be occasionally lost at sea during their migrations, but, so far as I know, they are not preyed upon by any other species.

The valley of the Hudson, I find, forms a great natural highway for the birds, as do doubtless the Connecticut, the Susquehanna, the Delaware, and all other large water courses running north and south. The birds love an easy way, and in the valleys of the rivers they find a road already graded for them ; and they abound more in such places throughout the season than they do further inland. The swarms of robins that come to us in early spring are a delight to behold. In one of his poems Emerson speaks of

" April's bird, Blue coated, flying before from tree to tree :"

but April's bird with me is the robin, brisk, vociferous, musical, dotting every field, and larking it in every grove; he is as easily atop at this season as the bobolink is a onth or two later. The tints of April are ruddy and brown—the new furrow and the leafless trees, and these are the tints of its dominant bird.

From my dining-room window I look, or did look, out upon a long stretch of smooth meadow, and as pretty a spring sight as I ever wish to behold was this field, sprinkled all over with robins, their red breasts turned toward the morning sun, or their pert forms sharply outlined against lingering patches of snow. Every morning for weeks I had those robins for breakfast; but what*they*had I never could find out.

After the leaves are out and gayer colours come into fashion, the robin takes a back seat. He goes to housekeeping in the old apple-tree, or, what he likes better, the cherry-tree. A pair reared their domestic altar (of mud and dry grass) in one of the latter trees, where I saw much of them. The cock took it upon himself to keep the tree free of all other robins during cherry-time, and its branches were the scene of some lively tussles every hour in the day. The innocent visitor would scarcely alight before the jealous cock was upon him; but while he was thrusting the intruder out at one side, a second would be coming in on he other. He managed, however, to protect his cherries very well, but had so little time to eat the fruit himself, that we got fully our share.

I have frequently seen the robin courting, and have always been astonished and amused at the utter coldness and indifference of the female. The females of every species of birds, however, I believe, have this in common—they are absolutely free from coquetry, or any airs and wiles whatever. In most cases nature has given the song and the plumage to the other sex, and all the embellishing and acting is done by the male bird.

I am always at home when I see the pas-senger-pigeon. Few spectacles please me more than to see clouds of these birds sweeping across the sky, and few sounds are more agreeable to my ear than their lively piping and calling in the spring woods. They come in such multitudes, they people the whole air; they cover townships, and make the solitary places gay as with a festival. The naked woods are suddenly blue as with fluttering ribbons and scarfs, and vocal as with the voices of children. Their arrival is always unexpected. We know April will bring the robins and May the obolinks, but we do not know that either they, or any other month, will bring the passenger-pigeon. Sometimes years elapse and scarcely a flock is seen. Then, of a sudden, some March or April they come pouring over the horizon from the south or south-west, and for a few days the land is alive with them.

The whole race seems to be collected in a few vast swarms or assemblages. Indeed, I have sometimes thought there was only one such in the United States, and that it moved in squads, and regiments, and brigades, and divisions, like a giant army. The scouting and foraging squads are not unusual, and every few years we see larger bodies of them, but rarely, indeed, do we witness the spectacle of the whole vast tribe in motion. Sometimes we hear of them in Virginia, or Kentucky and Tennessee; then in Ohio or Pennsylvania; then in New York, then in Canada or Michigan or Missouri. They are followed from point to point, and from State to State, by human sharks, who catch and shoot them for market.

A year ago last April, the pigeons flew for two or three days up and down the Hudson. In long bowing lines, or else in dense masses, they moved across the sky. It was not the hole army, but I should think at least one corps of it; I had not seen such a flight of pigeons since my boyhood. I went up to the top of the house, the better to behold the winged procession. The day seemed memorable and poetic in which such sights occurred.

While I was looking at the pigeons, a flock of wild geese went by, harrowing the sky northward. The geese strike a deeper chord than the pigeons. Level and straight they go as fate to its mark. I cannot tell what emotions these migrating birds awaken in me—the geese especially. One seldom sees more than a flock or two in a season, and what a spring token it is ! The great bodies are in motion. It is like the passage of a victorious army. No longer inch byinch does spring come, but these geese advance the standard across zones at one pull. How my desire goes with them; how something in me, wild and migratory, plumes itself and follows fast!

> " Steering north, with raucous cry,
> Through tracts and provinces of sky,
> Every night alighting down
> In new landscapes of romance,
> Where darkling feed the clamorous clans
> By lonely lakes to men unknown."

Dwelling upon these sights, I am reminded that the seeing of spring come not only upon the great wings of the geese and the lesser wings of the pigeons and birds, but in the many more subtle and indirect signs and mediums, is also a part of the compensation of living in the country. I enjoy not less what may be called the negative side of spring—those dark, dank, dissolving days— yellow sposh and mud and water everywhere,—yet who can stay long indoors? The humidity is soft and satisfying to the smell, and to the face and hands, and, for the first time for months, there is the fresh odour of the earth. The air is full of the notes and calls of the first birds. The domestic fowls refuse their accustomed food and wander far from the barn. Is it something winter has left, or spring has dropped, that they pick up? And what is it that holds me so long standing in the yard or in the fields? Something besides the ice and snow melts and runs away with the spring floods.

The little sparrows and purple finches are so punctual in announcing spring, that some seasons one wonders how they know without looking in the almanac, for surely there are no signs of spring out of doors. Yet theywill strike up as cheerily amid the driving snow as if they had just been told that tomorrow is the first day of March. About the same time I notice the potatoes in the cellar show signs of sprouting. They, too, find out so quickly when soring is near. Spring comes by two routes—in the air and Tinder ground, and often gets here by the latter course first. She undermines winter, when outwardly his front is nearly as bold as ever. I have known the trees to bud long before, by outward appearances, one would expect them to. The frost was gone from the ground before the snow was gone from the surface. But winter hath his birds also; some of them" such tiny bodies, that one wonders how they withstand the giant cold—but they do. J Birds live on highly concentrated food—the fine seeds of weeds and grasses, and the eggs and larvsæ of insects. Such food must be very stimulating and heating. A gizzard full of ants, for instance, what spiced and seasoned extract is equal to that? Think what virtue there must be in an ounce of gnats or mosquitoes, or in the fine mysterious food the chickadee and brown-creeper gather in the winter woods. It is doubtful if these birds ever freeze when fuel enough an be had to keep their little furnaces oing. And, as they get their food entirely rom the limbs and trunks of trees, like the ood-peckers, their supply is seldom interered with by the snow. The worst annoyance must be the enamelling of ice our inter woods sometimes get.

Indeed, the food question seems to be the only serious one with the birds. Give them plenty to eat, and, no doubt, the majority of them would face our winters. I believe all the woodpeckers are winter birds, except the high-hole or yellow-hammer, and he obtains the greater part of his subsistence from the ground, and is not a woodpecker at all in his habits of feeding. Were it not that it has recourse to budding, the ruffed grouse would be obliged to migrate. The quail, a bird, no doubt, equally hardy, but whose food is at the mercy of the snow, is frequently cnt off by our severe winters when it ventures to brave them, which is not often. Where plenty of the berries of the red cedar can be had, the cedar-bird will pass the winter in New York. The old ornithologists say the bluebird migrates to Bermuda; but in the winter of 1874-75, severe as it was, a pair of them wintered with me eighty miles north of New York city They seem to have been decided in their choice by the attractions of my rustic porch and the fruit of a sugar-berry tree (celtis—a kind of lotus) that stood in front of it. They lodged in the porch and took their meals in the tree. Indeed, they became regular lotus-eaters. Punctually at dusk they were in their places on a large laurel root in the top of the porch, whence, however, they were frequently routed by an indignant broom that was jealous of the neatness of the porch floor. But the pair would not take any hints of this kind, and did not give up their quarters in the porch or their lotus berries till spring.

Many times during the winter the sugar-berry tree was visited by a flock of cedar-birds that also wintered in the vicinity. At such times it was amusing to witness the pretty wrath of the bluebirds, scolding and threatening the intruders, and begrudging them every berry they ate. The bluebird cannot utter a harsh or unpleasing note. Indeed, he seems to have but one language, one speech, for both love and war, and the expression of his indignation is nearly as musical as his song. The male frequently made hostile demonstrations toward the cedar-birds, but did not openly attack them,and, with his mate, appeared to experience great relief when the poachers had gone.

l had other company in my solitude also, among the rest a distinguished arrival from the far north, the pine grossbeak,' a bird rarely seen in these parts, except now and then a single specimen.) But in the winter of 1875, heralding the extreme cold weather, and, no doubt, in consequence of it, there was a large incursion of them into this State and New England. They attracted the notice of the country people everywhere. I first saw them early in December about the head of the Delaware. I was walking along a cleared ridge with my gun, just at sundown, when I beheld two strange birds sitting in a small maple. On bringing one of them down, I found it was a bird I had never before seen ; in colour and shape like the purple finch, but quite as large again in size. From its heavy beak I at once recognised it as belonging to the family of gross-beaks. A few days later I saw large numbers of them in the woods, on the ground, and in the trees. And still later, and on till February, they were very numerous on the Hudson, coming all about my house—more familiar even than the little snow-bird, hopping beneath the windows, and looking up at me apparently with as much curiosity as I looked down upon them. They fed on the buds of the sugar-maples and upon frozen apples in the orchard. They were mostly young birds and females, coloured very much like the common sparrow, with now and then visible the dull carmine-coloured head and neck of an old male.

Other northern visitors that tarried with me the same winter were the tree or Canada sparrow and the red-poll, the former a bird larger "than the social sparrow, or hair-bird, but otherwise much resembling it, and "distinguishable by a dark spot in the middle of its breast; the latter a bird the size, and shape of the common gold-finch, with the same manner of flight and nearly the same note or cry. but darker than, the winter plumage of the goldfinch, and with a red crown and a tinge of red on the breast. Little bands of these two species lurked about the barn-yard all winter picking up the hay-seed, the sparrow sometimes venturing in on the hay-mow when the supply outside was short. I felt grateful to them for their company. They gave a sort of ornithological air to every errand I had to the barn.

Though a number of birds face our winters, and by various shifts worry through till spring, some of them permanent residents, and some of them visitors from the far north, yet there is but one genuine snowbird, nursling of the snow, and that is the snow-bunting, a bird that seems proper to this season,. heralding the coming storm, sweeping by on bold and rapid wing, and calling and chirping as cheerily as the songsters of May. In its plumage it reflects the winter landscape—an expanse of white surmounted or streaked with grey and brown; a field of snow with a line of woods or a tinge . of stubble. It fits into the scene, and does not appear to lead a beggarly and disconsolate life, like most of our winter residents. During the ice-harvesting on the river, I see them flitting about Among the gangs of men, or floating on the cakes of ice picking and scratching amid the dropping of the hdrses. They love the stack and hay-barn in the distant field, where the farmer fodders his cattle upon the snow, and every red root, rag-weed, or pig-weed left standing in the fall adds to their winter stores.

Though this bird, and one or two others, like the chickadee and nut-hatch, are more or less complacent and cheerful during the winter yet no bird can look our winters in , the face! and sing, as do so many of the English birds. Several species in Great Britain, their biographers tell us, sing the winter through, except during the severest frosts; but with us as far south as Virginia, and, for aught I know, much further, the birds are tuneless at this season. The owls, even, do not hoot, nor the hawks scream.

Among the birds that tarry briefly with us in the spring on their way to Canada and beyond, there is none I behold with so much pleasure as the white-crowned sparrow. ,'I have an eye out for him all through April and the first week in May. He is the rarest and most beautiful of the sparrow kind. He is crowned as some hero or victor in the games. He is usually in company with his congener, the white-throated sparrow, but seldom more than in the proportion of one to twenty 'of the latter. Contrasted with this bird, he looks like its more fortunate brother, upon whom some special distinction has been conferred, and who is, from the egg, of finer make and quality. His sparrow colour of ashen grey and brown is very clear and bright, and his form graceful. His whole expression, however, culminates I in a singular manner in his crown. The various tints of the bird are brought to a focus here and intensified, the lighter ones becoming white, and the deeper ones nearly black. There is the suggestion of a crest also, from a habit the bird has of slightly elevating this part of its plumage, as if to make more conspicuous its pretty markings. They are great scratchers, and will often remain several minutes scratching in one place, like a hen. Yet, unlike the hen and like all hoppers, they scratch with both feet at once, which is by no means the best way to scratch.

The white-throats often sing during their sojourning in both fall and spring; but only on one occasion have I ever heard any part of the song of the white-crowned, and that proceeded from what I took to be a young male, one October morning, just as the sun was rising. It was pitched very low, like a half-forgotten air, but it was very sweet. It was the song of the vesper-sparrow and the white-throat in one. In his breeding haunts he must be a superior songster, but he is very chary of his music while on his travels. The sparrows are all meek and lowly birds 1 They are of the grass, the fences, the low bushes, the weedy wayside places. Nature has denied them all brilliant tints, but she has given them sweet and musical voices. Theirs are the quaint and simple lullaby songs of childhood. The white-throat has a timid, tremulous strain, that issues from the low bushes or from behind the fence, where its cradle is hid. The song-sparrow modulates its simple ditty as softly as the lining of its own nest. The vesper-sparrow has only peace and gentleness in its strain.

What pretty nests, too, the sparrows build! Can anything be more exquisite than a sparrow's nest under a grassy or mossy bank ? What care the bird has taken not to disturb one straw or spear of grass, or thread of moss ! You cannot approach it and put your hand in to it without violating the place more or less, and yet the little architect has wrought day after day and left no marks. There has been an excavation, and yet no grain of earth appears to have been moved. If the nest had slowly and silently grown like the grass and the moss, it could not have been more nicely adjusted to its place and surroundings. There is absolutely nothing to tell the eye it is there. Generally a few spears of dry grass fall down from the turf above and form a slight screen before it. How commonly and coarsely it begins, blending with the débris that lies about, and how it refines and comes into form as it approaches the centre, which is modelled so perfectly and lined so softly ! Then, when the full complement of eggs is laid, and nidification has fairly begun, what a sweet, pleasing little mystery the silent old bank holds !

The song-sparrow, whose nest I have been describing, displays a more marked individuality in its song than any bird with which I am acquainted. Birds of the same species generally all sing alike, but I have observed numerous song-sparrows with songs peculiarly their own. Last season, the whole summer through, one sang about my grounds like this swee-e-tt *swee-e-t, sivee-e-t, bitter*. Day after day, from May to September, I heard this strain, which I thought a simple, but very profound summing-up of life, and wondered how the little bird had learned it so quickly. The present season, I heard another with a song equally original, but not so easily worded. Among a large troop of them in April, my attention was attracted to one that was a master songster—some Shelley or Tennyson among his kind. The strain was remarkably prolonged, intricate, and animated, and far surpassed anything I ever before heard from that source.

But the most noticeable instance o departure from the standard song of a species I ever knew of, was in the case of a wood-thrush. The bird sang, as did the sparrow, the whole season through, at the foot of my lot near the river. The song began correctly and ended correctly; but, interjected into it about midway, was a- loud, piercing, artificial note, at utter variance with the rest of the strain When my ear first caught this singular note, I started out, not a little puzzled, to make, as I supposed, a new acquaintance, but had not gone far when I discovered whence it proceeded. Brass amid gold, or pebbles amid pearls, are not more out of place than was this discordant scream or cry in the melodious strain of the wood-thrush. It pained and startled the ear. It seemed as if the instrument of the bird was not under control, or else that one note was sadly out of tune, and, when its turn came, instead of giving forth one of those sounds that are indeed like pearls, it shocked the ear with a piercing discord. Yet the singer appeared entirely unconscious of the defect; or had he grown used to it, or had his friends persuaded him that it was a variation to be coveted? Sometimes, after the brood had hatched and the bird's pride was at its full, he would make a little triumphal tour of the locality, coming from under the hill quite up to the house and flaunting his cracked instrument in the face of whoever would listen. He did not return again the next season; or, if he did, the malformation of his song was gone.

I have noticed that the bobolink does not sing the same in different localities. In New Jersey it has one song; on the Hudson a slight variation of the same, and on the high grass lands of the interior of the State quite a different strain,—clearer, more distinctly articulated, and running off with more sparkle and liltingness. It reminds one of the clearer mountain air and the translucent spring water of those localities. I never could make out what the bobolink says in New Jersey, but in certain districts in this State his enunciation is quite distinct. Sometimes he begins with the word **gegue, gegue**. Then again, more fully, **be true to me, Clarsy, be true to me, Clarsy, Clarsy,** thence full tilt into his inimitable song, interspersed in which the words **kick your slipper, kick your slipper,** and **temperance, temperance** (the last with a peculiar nasal resonance), are plainly heard. At its best, it is a remarkable performance, a unique performance, as it contains not the slightest hint or suggestion, either in tone, or manner, or effect, of any other bird-song to be heard. The bobolink has no mate or parallel in any of the world. He stands alone. There no closely allied species. He is not a lark, nor a finch, nor a warbler, nor a thrush, nor a starling (though classed with the starlings by late naturalists). He is an exception to many well-known rules. He is the only ground-bird known to me of marked and conspicuous plumage. He is the only black-and-white bird we have east of the Mississippi, and what is still more odd, he is black beneath and white above— the reverse of the fact in all other cases. Pre-eminently a bird of the meadow during the breeding season, and associated with clover, and daisies, and buttercups, as no other bird is, he yet has the look of an interloper or a new-comer, and not of one to the manor born.

The bobolink has an unusually full throat, which may help account for his great power of song. No bird has yet been found that could imitate him, or even repeat or suggest a single note, as if his song were the product of a new set of organs. There is a vibration about it and a rapid running over the keys that is the despair of other songsters. It is said that the mocking-bird is dumb in the presence of the bobolink. My neighbour has an English skylark that was hatched and reared in captivity. The bird is a most persistent and vociferous songster, and fully as successful a mimic as the mocking-bird. It pours out a strain that is a regular mosaic of nearly all the bird-notes to be heard, its own proper lark song forming a kind of bordering for the whole. The notes of the phcebebird, the purple finch, the swallow, the yellow-bird, the king-bird, the robin, and others, are rendered with perfect distinctness and accuracy, but not a word of the bobolink's, though the lark must have heard its song every day for four successive summers. It was the one conspicuous note in the fields around that the lark made no attempt to plagiarise. He could not steal the bobolink's thunder.

The lark is only a more marvellous song- -ster than the bobolink on account of his soaring flight, and the sustained copiousness of his song. His note is rasping and harsh, in point of melody, when compared with the bobolink's. When caged and near at hand the lark's song is positively disagreeable ; it is so loud and full of sharp, aspirated sounds. But high in air above the broad downs, poured out without interruption for many minutes together, it is very agreeable.

The bird among us that is usually called a lark, namely, the meadow-lark, but which our later classifiers say is no lark at all, has nearly the same quality el voice as the English skylark—loud, piercing, z-z-ing ; and during the mating season it frequently indulges while on the wing in a brief song that is quite lark-like. It is also a bird of the stubble, and one of the last to retreat on the approach of winter. The habits of many of our birds are slowly undergoing a change. Their migrations are less marked. With the settlement and cultivation of the country the means of subsistence of nearly every species are vastly increased. Insects are more numerous, and seeds of weeds and grasses more abundant. They become more and more domestic like the English birds. The swallows have nearly all left their original abodes,—hollow trees, and cliffs, and rocks,—for human, habitations and their environments. Where did the barn-swallow nest before the country was settled ? The chimney-swallow nested in hollow trees, and, perhaps, occasionally resorta thither yet. But the chimney, notwithstanding the smoke, seems to suit his taste best. In the spring, before they have paired, I think these swallows sometimes pass the night in the woods, but not if an old disused chimney is handy.

One evening in early May my attention was arrested by a band of them containing several hundred, perhaps a thousand, circling about near a large, tall, disused chimney in a secluded place in the country. They were very lively, and chippering, and diving in a most extraordinary manner. They formed a broad continuous circle many rods in diameter. Gradually the circle contracted and neared the chimney. Presently some of the birds as they came round began to dive toward it, and the chippering was more animated than ever. Then a few ventured in; in a moment more, the air at the mouth of the chimney was black with the stream of descending swallows. When the passage began to get crowded, the circle lifted and the rest of the birds continued their flight, giving those inside time to dispose of themselves. Then the influx began again, and was kept up till the crowd became too great, when it cleared as before. Thus by instalments, or in layers, the swallows were packed into the chimney until the last one was stowed away. Passing by the place a few days afterward, I saw a board reaching from the roof of the building to the top of the chimney, and imagined some curious person or some predaceous boy had been up to take a peep inside, and see how so many swallows could dispose of themselves in such a space. It would have been an interesting spectacle to see them emerge from the chimney in the morning.

APRIL.

If we represent the winter of our northern climate by a rugged snow-clad mountain, and summer by a broad fertile plain, then the intermediate belt, the hilly and breezy uplands, will stand for spring, with March reaching well up into the region of the snows, and April lapping well down upon the greening fields and unloosened currents, not beyond the limits of winter's sallying storms, but well within the vernal zone,— within the reach of the warm breath and subtle, quickening influences of the plain below. At its best, April is the tenderest of tender salads made crisp by ice or snow water. Its type is the first spear of grass. The senses—sight, hearing, smell—are as hungry for its delicate and almost spiritual tokens, as the cattle are for the first bite of its fields. How it touches one and makes him both glad and sad ! The voices of the arriving birds, the migrating fowls, the clouds of pigeons sweeping across the sky or filling the woods, the elfin horn of the first honey-bee venturing abroad in the middle of the day, the clear piping of the little frogs in the marshes at sundown, the camp-fire in the sugar-bush, the smoke seen afar rising over the trees, the tinge of green that comes SO suddenly on the sunny knolls and slopes, the full translucent streams, the waxing and warming sun,—how these things and others like them are noted by the eager eye and ear! April is my natal month, and I am born again into new delight and new surprises at each return of it. Its name has an indescribable charm to me. Its two syllables are like the calls of the first birds—like that of the phoebe-bird, or of the meadow-lark. Its very snows are fertilising, and are called the poor man's manure.

Then its odours! I am thrilled by its fresh and indescribable odours—the perfume of the bursting sod, of the quickened roots and rootlets, of the mould under the leaves, of the fresh furrows. No other month has odours like it. The west wind the other day came fraught with a perfume that was to the sense of smell what a wild and delicate strain of music is to the ear. It was almost transcendental. I walked across the hill with my nose in the air taking it in. It lasted for two days. I imagined it came from the willows of a distant swamp, whose catkins were affording the bees their first pollen,—or did it come from much further— from beyond the horizon, the accumulated breath of innumerable farms and budding forests? The main characteristic of these April odours is their uncloying freshness. They are not sweet, they are oftener bitter, they are penetrating and lyrical. I know well the odours of May and June, of the world of meadows and orchards bursting into bloom, but they are not so ineffable and immaterial and so stimulating to the sense as the incense of April.

The season of which I speak does not correspond with the April of the almanac in all sections of our vast geography. It answers to March in Virginia and Maryland, while in parts of New York and New England it laps well over into May. It begins when the partridge drums, when the hyla pipes, when the shad start up the rivers, when the grass greens in the spring runs, and it ends when the leaves are unfolding and the last snow-flake dissolves in mid-air. It is the first of May when the first swallow appears, when the whip-poor-will is heard, when the wood-thrush sings, but it is April as long as there is snow upon the mountains, no matter what the almanac may say. Our April is, in fact a kind of Alpine summer, full of such contrasts and touches of wild, delicate beauty as no other season affords. The deluded citizen fancies there is nothing enjoyable in the country till June, and so misses the freshest, tenderest part. It is as if one should miss strawberries and begin his fruit eating with melons and peaches. These last are good—supremely so, they are melting and luscious, but nothing so thrills and penetrates the tastes and wakes up and teases the papillæ of the tongue as the uncloying strawberry. What midsummer sweetness half so distracting as its brisk sub-acid flavour, and what splendour of full-leaved June can stir the blood like the best of leafless April ?

One characteristic April feature, and (Me that delights me very much, is the perfect emerald of the spring runs while the fields are yet brown and sere,—strips and patches of the most vivid velvet green on the slopes and in the valleys. How the eye grazes there and is filled and refreshed? I had forgotten what a marked feature this was until I recently rode in an open wagon for three days through a mountainous, pastoral country, remarkable for its fine springs. Those delicious green patches are yet in my eye. The fountains flowed with May. Where no springs occurred, there were hints and suggestions of springs about the fields and by the road-side in the freshened grass— sometimes overflowing a space in the form of an actual fountain. The water did not quite get to the surface in such places, but sent its influence.

The fields of wheat and rye, too, how they stand out of the April landscape— great green squares on a field of brown or grey !

Among April sounds there is none more welcome or suggestive to me than the voice of the little frogs piping in the marshes. No bird-note can surpass it as a spring token; and as it is not mentioned, to my knowledge, by the poets and writers of other lands, I am ready to believe it is characteristic of our season alone. You may be sure April has really come when this little amphibian creeps out of the mud and inflates its throat. We talk of the bird inflating its throat, but you should see this tiny minstrel inflate its throat, which becomes like a large bubble, and suggests a drummer-boy with his drum slung very high. In this drum, or by the aid of it, the sound is produced. Generally the note is very feeble at first, as if the frost was not yet all out of the creature's throat, and only one voice will be heard, some prophet bolder than all the rest, or upon whom the quickening ray of spring has first fallen. And it often happens that he is stoned for his pains by the yet unpacified element, and is compelled literally to " shut up " beneath a fall of snow or a heavy frost. Soon, however, he lifts up his voice again with more confidence, and is joined by others and still others, till in due time, say toward the last of the month, there is a shrill musical uproar, as the sun is setting, in every marsh and bog in the land. It is a plaintive sound, and I have heard people from the city speak of it as lonesome and depressing, but to the lover of the country it is a pure spring melody. The little piper will sometimes climb a bulrush, to which he clings like a sailor to a mast, and sends forth his shrill call. There is a southern species heard when you have reached the Potomac whose note is far more harsh and crackling. To stand on the verge of a swamp vocal with these, pains and stuns the ear. The call of the northern species is far more tender and musical. There is yet in my mind some uncertainty about the truth of the opinion held by naturalists, that

these little frogs presently take to the trees and become the well-known " tree-toads " whose call so frequently announces rain.

Then is there anything like a perfect April morning ? One hardly knows what the sentiment of it is, but it is something very delicious. It is youth and hope. It is a new earth and a new sky. How the air transmits sounds, and what an awakening, prophetic character all sounds have! The distant barking of a dog, or the lowing of a cow, or the crowing of a cock seems from out the heart of Nature, and to be a call to come forth. The great sun appears to have been reburnished, and there is something in his first glance above the eastern hills, and the way his eye-beams dart right and left and smite the rugged mountains into gold, that quickens the pulse and inspires the heart.

Across the fields in the early morning I hear some of the rare April birds—the chee-wink and the brown thrasher. The robin, bluebird, song-sparrow, phcebe-bird, etc., come in March ; but these two ground birds are seldom heard till toward the last of April The ground birds are all tree-singers or air-singers; they must have an elevated stage to speak from. Our long-tailed thrush, or thrasher, like its congeners the cat-bird and mocking-bird, delights in a high branch of some solitary tree whence it will pour out its rich and intricate warble for an hour together. This bird is the great American chipper. There is no other bird that I know of that can chip with such emphasis and military decision as this yellow-eyed songster. It is like the click of a giant gun-lock. Why is the thrasher so stealthy? It always seems to be going about on tiptoe. I never knew it to steal anything, and yet it skulks and hides like a fugitive from justice. One never sees it flying aloft in the air, and traversing the world openly, like most birds, but it darts along fences and through bushes as if pursued by a guilty conscience. Only when the musical fit is upon it does it come up into full view, and invite the world to hear and behold.

The cheewink is a shy bird also, but not stealthy. It is very inquisitive, and sets up a great scratching among the leaves, apparently to attract your attention. The male is perhaps the most conspicuously marked of all the ground birds except the bobolink, being black above, bay on the sides, and white beneath. The bay is in compliment to the leaves he is for ever scratching among, — they have rustled against his breast and sides so long that these parts have taken their colour; but whence come the white and black? The bird seems to be aware that his colour betrays him, for there are few birds in the woods so careful about keeping themselves screened from view. When in song, its favourite perch is the top of some high bush near to cover. On being disturbed at such times it pitches down into the brush, and is instantly lost to view.

This is the bird that Thomas Jefferson wrote to Wilson about, greatly exciting the latter's curiosity. Wilson was just then upon the threshold of his career as an ornithologist, and had made a drawing of the Canada jay, which he sent to the President. It was a new bird, and, in reply, Jefferson called his attention to a "curious bird" which was everywhere to be heard, but scarcely ever to be seen. He had for twenty years interested the young sportsmen of his neighbourhood to shoot one for him, but without success. "It is in all the forests, from spring to fall," he says in his letter, "and never but on the tops of the tallest trees, from which it perpetually serenades us with some of the sweetest notes, and as clear as those of the nightingale. I have followed it for miles, without ever but once getting a good view of it.

It is of the size and make of the mocking-bird, lightly thrush-coloured on the back, and a greyish white on the breast and belly. Mr. Randolph, my son-in-law, was in possession of one which had been shot by a neighbour," etc. Randolph pronounced it a fly-catcher, which was a good way wide of the mark. Jefferson must have seen only the female, after all his tramp, from his description of the colour; but he was doubtless following his own great thoughts more than the bird, else he would have had an earlier view. The bird was not a new one, but was well known then as the ground-robin. The President put Wilson on the wrong scent by his erroneous description, and it was a long time before the latter got at the truth of the case. But Jefferson's letter is a good sample of those which specialists often receive from intelligent persons who have seen or heard something in their line, very curious, or entirely new, and who set the man of science agog by a description of the supposed novelty,—a description that generally fits the facts of the case about as well as your coat fits the chair-back. Strange and curious things in the air, and in the water, and in the earth beneath, are seen every day except by those who are looking for them, namely, the naturalists. When Wilson or Audubon gets his eye on the unknown bird, the illusion vanishes, and your phenomenon turns out. to be one of the commonplaces of the fields or woods.

A prominent April bird that one does not have to go to the woods or away from his own door to see and hear is the hardy, and ever-welcome meadow-lark. What a twang there is about this bird, and what vigour! It smacks of the soil. It is the winged embodiment of the spirit of our spring meadows. What emphasis in its *"z-d-t, z-d-t,"* and what character in its long, piercing note. Its straight, tapering, sharp beak is typical of its voice. Its note goes like a shaft from a cross-bow; it is a little too sharp and piercing when near at hand, but heard in the proper perspective, it is eminently melodious and pleasing. It is one of the major notes of the fields at this season. In fact, it easily dominates all others. *"Spring o the year! spring o the year"* it says, with a long-drawn breath, a little plaintive, but not complaining, or melancholy. At times it indulges in something much more intricate and lark-like while hovering on the wing in mid-air, but a song is beyond the compass of its instrument, and the attempt usually ends in a breakdown. A clear, sweet, strong, high-keyed note, uttered from some knoll, or rock, or stake in the fence, is its proper vocal performance. It has the build, and walk, and flight of the quail and the grouse. It gets up before you in much the same manner, and falls an easy prey to the crack shot. Its yellow breast, surmounted by a black crescent, it need not be ashamed to turn to the morning sun, while its coat of mottled grey is in perfect keeping with the stubble amid which it walks.

The two lateral white quills in its tail seem strictly in character. These quills spring from a dash of scorn and defiance in the bird's make-up. By the aid of these it can almost emit a flash as it struts about the fields and jerks out its sharp notes. They give a rayed, a definite and piquant expression to its movements. This bird is not properly a lark, but a starling, say the ornithologists, though it is lark-like in its habits, being a walker and entirely a ground bird. Its colour also allies it to the true lark. I believe there is no bird in the English or European fields that answers to this hardy pedestrian of our meadows. He is a true American, and his note one of our characteristic April sounds.

Another marked April note, proceeding sometimes from the meadows, but more frequently from the rough pastures and borders of the woods, is the call of the high-hole, or golden-shafted woodpecker. It is quite as strong as that of the mead-ow-lark, but not so long-drawn and piercing. It is a succession of short notes rapidly uttered, as if the bird said, *"if-if-if-if4f-if-if."* The note of the ordinary downy, or hairy woodpecker, suggests, in some way, the sound of a steel punch; but that of the high-hole is much softer, and strikes on the ear with real spring-time melody. The high-hole is not so much a woodpecker as he is a ground-pecker. He subsists largely on ants and crickets, and does not appear till they are to be found.

In Solomon's description of spring the voice of the turtle is prominent, but our turtle, or mourning dove, though it arrives in April, can hardly be said to contribute noticeably to the open-air sounds. Its call is so vague, and soft, and mournful,—in fact, so remote and diffused, that few persons ever hear it at all.

Such songsters as the cow blackbird are noticeable at this season, though they take a back seat a little later. It utters a peculiarly liquid April sound. Indeed, one would think its crop was full of water, its notes so bubble up and regurgitate, and are delivered with such an apparent stomachic contraction. This bird is the only feathered polygamist we have. The females are greatly in excess of the males, and the latter are usually attended by three or four of the former. As soon as the other birds begin to build, they are on the qui vive, prowling about like gypsies, not to steal the young of others, but. to steal their eggs into other birds' nests, and so shirk the labour and responsibility of hatching and rearing their own young. As these birds do not mate, and as therefore there can be little or no rivalry or competition between the males, one wonders—in view of Darwin's teaching —why one sex should have brighter and richer plumage than the other, which is the fact. The males are easily distinguished from the dull and faded females by their deep, glossy, black coats.

The April of English literature corresponds nearly to our May. In Great Britain the swallow and the cuckoo arrive in April; with us, their appearance is several weeks later. Our April, at its best, is a bright laughing face under a hood of snow like the English March, but presenting sharper contrasts, a greater mixture of smiles and tears and icy looks than are known to our ancestral climate. Indeed, winter sometimes retraces his steps in this month, and unburdens himself of the snows that the previous cold has kept back; but we are always sure of a number of radiant, equable days— days that go before the bud when the sun embraces the earth with fervour and determination. How his beams pour into the woods till the mould under the leaves is warm and emits an odour ! The waters glint and sparkle, the birds gather in groups, and even those unwont to sing find a voice. On the streets of the cities, what a flutter, what bright looks and gay colours ! I recall one pre-eminent day of this kind last April. I made a note of it in my notebook. The earth seemed suddenly to emerge from a wilderness of clouds and chilliness into one of these blue sunlit spaces. How the voyagers rejoiced ! Invalids came forth, old men sauntered down the street, stocks went up, and the political outlook brightened.

Such days bring out the last of the hiber-. nating animals. The woodchuck unrolls and creeps out of his den to see if his clover has started yet. The torpidity leaves the snakes and the turtles, and they come forth and bask in the sun. There is nothing so small, nothing so great, that it does not respond to these celestial spring days, and give the pendulum of life a fresh start.

April is also the month of the new furrow. As soon as the frost is gone and the ground settled, the plough is started upon the hill, and at each bout I see its brightened mould-board flash in the sun. Where the last remnants of the snow-drift lingered yesterday the plough breaks the sod to-day. Where the drift was deepest the grass is pressed flat, and there is a deposit of sand and earth blown from the fields to windward. Line upon line the turf is reversed, until there stands out of the neutral landscape a ruddy square visible for miles, or until the breasts of the broad hills glow like the breasts of the robins.

Then who would not have a garden in April? to rake together the rubbish and burn it up, to turn over the renewed soil, to scatter the rich compost, to plant the first seed, or bury the first tuber ! It is not the seed that is planted, any more than it is I that is planted ; it is not the dry stalks and weeds that are burned up, any more than it is my gloom and regrets that are consumed. An April smoke makes a clean harvest.

I think April is the best month to be born in. One is just in time, so to speak, to catch the first train which is made up in this month. My April chickens always turn out best. They get an early start; they have rugged constitutions. Late chickens cannot stand the heavy dews, or withstand the predaceous hawks. In April all nature starts with you. You have not come out your hibernaculum too early or too late; the time is ripe, and if you do not keep pace with the rest, why, the fault is not in the season.

SPRING POEMS.

There is no month oftener on the tongues of the poets than April. It is the initiative month ; it opens the door of the seasons; the interest and expectations of the untried, the untasted, lurk in it.

" From you have I been absent in the spring,"

says Shakespeare in one of his sonnets,
" When proud-pied April, dressed in all his trim,
Hath put a spirit of youth in everything,
That heavy Saturn laughed and leaped with him."

The following poem from Tennyson's "In Memoriam " might be headed " April," and serve as descriptive of parts of our season :—

" Now fades the last long streak of snow,
Now bourgeons every maze of quick About the flowering squares, and thick By ashen roots the violets blow.

Now rings the woodland loud and long
The distance takes a lovelier hue,
And drown'd in yonder living blue
The lark becomes a sightless song.

Now dance the lights on lawn and lea,
The flocks are whiter down the vale,
And milkier every milky sail
On winding stream or distant sea;

Where now the sea-mew pipes, or dives
In yonder greening gleam, and fly
The happy birds, that change their sky
To build and brood; that live their lives

From land to land; and in my breast
Spring wakens too; and my regret
Becomes an April violet,
And buds and blossoms like the rest."

In the same poem the poet asks :—

" Can trouble live with April days ?"

Yet they are not all jubilant chords that this season awakens. Occasionally there is an undertone of vague longing and sadness, akin to that which one experiences in autumn. Hope for a moment assumes the attitude of memory and stands with reverted look. The haze that in spring as well as in fall sometimes descends and envelops all things, has in it in some way the sentiment of music, of melody, and awakens pensive thoughts. Elizabeth Akers, in her " April," has recognised and fully expressed this feeling. I give the first and last stanzas :—

" The strange, sweet days are here again
The happy-mournful days;
The songs which trembled on our lips
Are half complaint, half praise.

Swing, robin, on the budded sprays,
And sing your blithest tune;—
Help us across these homesick days
Into the joy of June !"

This poet has also given a touch of spring in her "March," which, however, should be written "April" in the New England climate.

" The brown buds thicken on the trees,
Unbound the free streams sing,
As March leads forth across the leas
The wild and windy spring.

Where in the fields the melted snow
Leaves hollows warm and wet,
Ere many days will sweetly blow
The first blue violet."

But on the whole the poets have not been eminently successful in depicting spring. The humid season with its tender melting blue sky, its fresh earthly smells, its new furrow, its few simple signs and awakenings here and there, and its strange feeling of unrest,—how difficult to put its charms into words? None of the so-called pastoral poets have succeeded in doing it. That is the best part of spring which escapes a direct and matter-of-fact description of her. There is more of spring in a line or two of Chaucer and Spenser than in the elaborate portraits of her by Thomson or Pope, because the former had spring in their hearts, and the latter only in their inkhorns. Nearly all Shakespeare's songs are spring-songs—full of the banter, the frolic, and the love-making of the early season. What an unloosed current, too, of joy and fresh new life and appetite in Burns!

In spring everything has such a margin; there are such spaces of silence. The influences are at work underground. Our delight is in a few things. The drying road is enough; a single wild-flower, the note of the first bird, the partridge drumming in the April woods, the restless herds, the sheep steering for the uplands, the cow lowing in the highway or hiding her calf in the bushes, the first fires, the smoke going up through the shining atmosphere, from the burning of rubbish in gardens and old fields, etc., each of these simple things fills the breast with yearning and delight, for they are tokens of the spring. The best spring-poems have this singleness and sparse-ness. Listen to Solomon: "For lo, the winter is past, the rain is over and gone; the flowers appear on the earth; the time of the singing of birds is come, and the voice of the turtle is heard in our land." In Wordsworth are some things that breathe the air of spring. These lines, written in early spring, afford a good specimen :—

" I heard a thousand blended notes,
While in a grove I sat reclined,
In that sweet mood when pleasant thoughts
Bring sad thoughts to the mind.

To her fair works did Nature link

The human soul that through me ran;
And much it grieved my heart to think
What man has made of man.

Through primrose tufts, in that green bower,
The periwinkle trailed its wreaths;
And 'tis my faith that every flower
Enjoys the air it breathes.

The birds around me hopped and played,
Their thoughts I cannot measure :—
But the least motion which they made,
It seemed a thrill of pleasure."

Or these, from another poem written in his usual study, Out-of-Doors, and addressed to his sister:—

" It is the first mild day of March :
Each minute sweeter than before
The redbreast sings from the tall larch
That stands beside our door.

There is a blessing in the air,
Which seems a sense of joy to yield
To the bare trees, and mountains bare,
And grass in the green field

Love, now a universal birth,
From heart to heart is stealing,
From earth to man, from man to earth :
--It is the hour of feeling.

One moment now may give us more

Than fifty years of reason :
Our minds shall drink at every pore
The spirit of the season."

It is the simplicity of such lines, like the naked branches of the trees or the unclothed fields, and the spring-like depth of feeling and suggestion they hold, that make them so appropriate to this season.

At this season I often find myself repeating these lines of his also :—

" My heart leaps up, when I behold
A rainbow in the sky:
So was it when my life began;
So is it now I am a man;
So be it when I shall grow old,
Or let me die !"

Though there are so few good poems especially commemorative of the spring, there have, no doubt, been spring-poets— poets with such newness and fulness of life and such quickening power, that the world is re-created, as it were, beneath their touch. Of course this is in a measure so with all real poets. But the difference I would indicate may exist between poets of the same or nearly the same magnitude. Thus, in this light, Tennyson is an autumnal poet, mellow and dead-ripe, and was so from the first, while Wordsworth has much more of the spring in him, is nearer the bone of things and to primitive conditions.

Among the old poems, one which seems to me to have much of the charm of springtime upon it is the story of Cupid and Psyche in Apuleius. The songs, gambols, and wooings of the early birds are not more welcome and suggestive. How graceful and airy, and yet what a tender, profound, human significance it contains ! But the great vernal poem, doubly so in that it is the expression of the spring-time of the race, the boyhood of man as well, is the Iliad of Homer. What faith, what simple wonder, what unconscious strength, what beautiful savagery, what magnanimous enmity—a very paradise of war !

Though so young a people, there is not much of the feeling of spring in any of our books. The muse of our poets is wise rather than joyous. There is no excess or extravagance or unruliness in her. There are spring sounds and tokens in Emerson's " May Day:"—

'April cold with dropping rain
Willows and lilacs brings again,
The whistle of returning birds,
And trumpet-lowing of the herds.
The scarlet maple-keys betray
What potent blood hath modest May;
What fiery force the earth renews,
The wealth of forms the flush of hues;
Joy shed in rosy waves abroad
Flows from the heart of Love, the Lord."

But this is not spring in the blood. Among the works of our young and. rising poets, I am not certain but Mr. Gilder's " New Day " is entitled to rank as a spring poem in the sense in which I am speaking. It is full of gaiety and daring, and full of the reckless abandon of the male bird when he is winning his mate. It is full also of the tantalising suggestiveness the half lights and shades of April and May.

Of prose-poets who have the charm of the spring-time upon them, the best recent example I know of is Björnson, the Norwegian romancist. What especially makes his books spring-like is their freshness and sweet good faith. There is also a reticence and an un-wrought suggestiveness about them that is like the promise of buds and early flowers. Of Turgeneiff, the Russian, much the same thing might be said. His stories are simple and elementary, and have none of the elaborate hair-splitting and forced hot-house character of the current English or American novel. They spring from stronger, more healthful and manly conditions, and have a force in them that is like a rising, incoming tide.

OUR RURAL DIVINITY.

I WONDER that Wilson Flagg did not include the cow among his Picturesque Animals, for that is where she belongs. She has not the classic beauty of the horse, but in picture-making qualities she is far ahead of him. Her shaggy, loose-jointed body, her irregular, sketchy outlines, like those of the landscape—the hollows and ridges, the slopes and prominences—her tossing horns, her bushy tail, her swinging gait, her tranquil, ruminating habits—all tend to make her an object upon which the artist eye loves to dwell. The artists are for ever putting her into pictures, too. In rural landscape scenes she is an important feature. Behold her grazing in the pastures and on the hill-sides, or along banks of streams, or ruminating under wide-spreading trees, or standing belly deep in the creek or pond, or lying upon the smooth places in the quiet summer afternoon, the day's grazing done, and waiting to be summoned home to be milked; and again in the twilight lying upon the level summit of the hill, or where the sward is thickest and softest; or in winter a herd of them filing along toward the spring to drink, or being "foddered" from the stack in the field upon the new snow — surely the cow is a picturesque animal, and all her goings and comings are pleasant to behold.

I looked into Hamerton's clever book on the domestic animals, also expecting to find my divinity duly celebrated, but he passes her by and contemplates the bo-vine qualities only as they appear in the ox and the bull.

Neither have the poets made much of the cow, but have rather dwelt upon the steer, or the ox yoked to the plough. I recall this touch from Emerson :—

" The heifer that lows in the upland farm,
Far heard, lows not thine ear to charm."

But the ear is charmed, nevertheless, especially if it be not too near, and the air be still and dense, or hollow, as the farmer says. And again, if it be spring-time, and she task that powerful bellows of hers to its utmost capacity, how round the sound is, and how far it goes over the hills.

The cow has at least four tones or lows. First, there is her alarmed or distressed low, when deprived of her calf, or separated from her mates—her low of affection. Then there is her call of hunger, a petition for food, sometimes full of impatience, or her answer to the farmer's call, full of eagerness. Then there is that peculiar frenzied bawl she utters on smelling blood, which causes every member of the herd to lift its head and hasten to the spot—the native cry of the clan. When she is gored or in great danger she bawls also, but that is different. And lastly, there is the long, sonorous volley she lets off on the hills, or in the yard, or along the highway, and which seems to be expressive of a kind of unrest and vague longing— the longing of the imprisoned Io for her lost identity. She sends her voice forth so that every god on Mount Olympus can hear her plaint. She makes this sound in the morning, especially in the spring, as she goes forth to graze.

One of our rural poets, Myron Benton, whose verse often has the flavour of sweet cream, has written some lines called "Rumination," in which the cow is the principal figure, and with which I am permitted to adorn my theme. The poet first gives his attention to a little brook that "breaks its shallow gossip " at his feet and " drowns the oriole's voice : "

" But moveth not that wise and ancient cow,
Who chews her juicy cud so languid now
Beneath her favourite elm, whose drooping bough
Lulls all but inward vision, fast asleep:
But still, her tireless tail a pendulum sweep
Mysterious clockwork guides, and some hid pulley
Her drowsy cud, each moment, raises duly.
Of this great, wondrous world she has seen more
an you, my little brook, and cropped its store

Of succulent grass on many a mead and lawn;
And strayed to distant uplands in the dawn,
And she has had some dark experience

Of graceless man's ingratitude; and hence
Her ways have not been ways of pleasantness,
Nor all her paths of peace. But her distress
And grief she has lived past; your giddy round
Disturbs her not, for she is learned profound
In deep Brahminical philosophy.
She chews the cud of sweetest reverie
Above your wordly prattle, brooklet merry,
Oblivious of all things sublunary."

The cow figures in Grecian mythology, and in the Oriental literature is treated as a sacred animal. "The clouds are cows and the rain milk." I remember what Herodotus Bays of the Egyptians' worship of heifers and steers; and in the traditions of the Celtic nations the cow is regarded as a divinity. In Norse mythology the milk of the cow Andhumbla afforded nourishment to the Frost giants, and it was she that licked into being and into shape a god, the father of Odin. If anything could lick a god into shape, certainly the cow could do it. You may see her perform this office for young Taurus any spring. She licks him out of the fogs and bewilderments and uncertainties in which he finds himself on first landing upon these shores, and up on to his feet in an incredibly short time. Indeed, that potent tongue of hers can almost make the dead alive any day, and the creative lick of the old Scandinavian mother cow is only a large-lettered rendering of the commonest facts.

The horse belongs to the fiery god Mars. He favours war, and is one of its oldest, most available, and most formidable engines. The steed is clothed with thunder, and smells the battle from afar; but the cattle upon a thousand hills denote that peace and plenty bear sway in the land. The neighing of the horse is a call to battle; but the lowing of old Brocklef ace in the valley brings the golden age again. The savage tribes are never without the horse; the Scythians are all mounted; but the cow would tame and humanise them. When the Indians will cultivate the cow, I shall think their civilisation fairly begun. Recently, when the horses were sick with the epizootic, and the oxen came to the city and helped to do their work, what an Arcadian air again filled the streets! But the dear old oxen—how awkward and distressed they looked! Juno wept in the face of every one of them. The horse is a true citizen, and is entirely at home in the paved streets ; but the ox—what a complete embodiment of all rustic and rural things ! Slow, deliberate, thick-skinned, powerful, hulky, ruminating, fragrant-breathed, when he came to town the spirit and suggestion of all Georgics and Bucolics came with him. 0 citizen, was it only a plodding, unsightly brute that went by? Was there no chord in your bosom, long silent, that sweetly vibrated at the sight of that patient, Herculean couple? Did you smell no hay or cropped herbage, see no summer pastures with circles of cool shade, hear no voice of herds among the hills ? They were very likely the only horses your grandfather ever had. Not much trouble to harness and unharness them. Not much vanity on the road in those days. They did all the work on the early pioneer farm. They were the gods whose rude strength first broke the soil. They could live where the moose and the deer could. If there was no clover or timothy to be had, then the twigs of the basswood and birch would do. Before there were yet fields given up to grass, they found ample pasturage in the woods. Their wide-spreading horns gleamed in the duskiness, and their paths and the paths of the cows became the future roads and highways, or even the streets of great cities.

All the descendants of Odin show a bovine trace, and cherish and cultivate the cow. In Norway she is a great feature. Prof. Boyesen describes what he calls the Setter, the spring migration of the dairy and dairymaids, with all the appurtenances of butter and cheese-making, from the valleys to the distant plains upon the mountains, where the grass keeps fresh and tender till fall. It is the great event of the year in all the rural districts. Nearly the whole family go with the cattle and remain with them. At evening the cows are summoned home with a long horn, called the loor, in the hands of the milkmaid. The whole herd comes winding down the mountain-side toward the Sætter in obedience to the mellow blast.

What were those old Vikings but thick-hided bulls that delighted in nothing so much as goring each other? And has not the charge of beefiness been brought much, nearer home to us than that? But about all the northern races there is something that is kindred to cattle in the best senses-something in their art and literature that is essentially pastoral, sweet-breathed, continent, dispassionate, ruminating, wide-eyed, soft-voiced—a charm of kine, the virtue of brutes.

The cow belongs more especially to the northern peoples, to the region of the good, green grass. She is the true grazing animal. That broad, smooth, always dewy nose of hers is just the suggestion of green sward. She caresses the grass; she sweeps off the ends of the leaves; she reaps it with the soft sickle of her tongue. She crops close, but she does not bruise or devour the turf like the horse. She is the sward's best friend, and will make it thick and smooth as a carpet.

" The turfy mountains where live the nibbling sheep"

are not for her. Her muzzle is too blunt; then she does not bite as do the sheep; she has not upper teeth; she crops. But on the lower slopes, and margins, and rich bottoms, she is at home. Where the daisy and the buttercup and clover bloom, and where corn will grow, is her proper domain. The agriculture of no country can long thrive without her. Not only a large part of the real, but much of the potential wealth of the land is wrapped up in her.

Then the cow has given us some good words and hints. How could we get along without the parable of the cow that gave a good pail of milk and then kicked it over. One could hardly keep house without it. Or the parable of the cream and the skimmed milk, or of the buttered bread ? We know, too, through her aid, what the horns of the dilemma mean, and what comfort there is in the juicy cud of reverie

I have said the cow has not been of much service to the poets, and yet I re-member that Jean Ingelow could hardly have managed her "High Tide" without "Whitefoot" and "Lightfoot" and "Cusha! Cusha! Cusha, calling;" or Trowbridge his " Evening at the Farm," in which the real call of the American farm-boy, of "Co', boss ! Co', boss! Co', Co ," makes a very musical refrain.

Tennyson's charming " Milking Song" is another flower of poesy that has sprung up in my divinity's footsteps.

What a variety of individualities a herd of cows presents when you have come to know them all, not only in form and colour, but in manners and disposition. Some are timid and awkward, and the butt of the whole herd. Some remind you of deer. Some have an expression in the face like certain persons you have known. A petted and well-fed cow has a benevolent and gracious look; an ill-used and poorly-fed one a pitiful and forlorn look. Some cows have a masculine or ox expression; others are extremely feminine. The latter are the ones for milk. Some cows will kick like a horse ; some jump fences like deer. Every herd has its ringleader, its unruly spirit—one that plans all the mischief, and leads the rest through the fences into the grain or into the orchard. This one is usually quite different from the master spirit, the "boss of the yard." The latter is generally the most peaceful and law-abiding cow in the lot, and the least bullying and quarrelsome. But she is not to be trifled with; her will is law; the whole herd give way before her, those that have crossed horns with her, and those that have not, but yielded their allegiance without crossing. I remember such a one among my father's milkers when I was a boy—a slender-horned, deep-shouldered, large-uddered, dewlapped old cow that we always put first in the long stable so she could not have a cow on each side of her to forage upon; for the master is yielded to no less in the stanchions than in the yard. She always had the first place anywhere. She had her choice of standing-room in the milking-yard, and when she wanted to lie down there or in the fields, the best and softest spot was hers. When the herd were foddered from the stack or barn, or fed with pumpkins in the fall, she was always first served. Her demeanour was quiet but impressive. She never bullied or gored her mates, but literally ruled them with the breath of her nostrils. If any new-comer or ambitious younger cow, however, chafed under her supremacy, she was ever ready to make good her claims. And with what spirit she would fight when openly challenged! She was a whirlwind of pluck and valour; and not after one defeat or two defeats would she yield the championship. The boss cow, when overcome, seems to brood over her disgrace, and day after day will meet her rival in fierce combat.

A friend of mine, a pastoral philosopher, whom I have consulted in regard to the master cow, thinks it is seldom the case that one rules all the herd, if it number many, but that there is often one that will rule nearly all. "Curiously enough," he says, "a case like this will often occur: No. 1 will whip No. 2; No. 2 whips No. 3, and No. 3 whips No. 1; so around in a circle. This is not a mistake; it is often the case. I remember," he continued, "we once had feeding out of a large bin in the centre of the yard six oxen who mastered right through in succession from No. 1 to No. 6 ; *but No. 6 paid off the score by whipping No* 1. I often watched them when they were all trying to feed out of the box, and of course trying, dog-in-the-manager fashion, each to prevent any other he could. They would often get in the order to do it very systematically, since they could keep rotating about the box till the chain happened to get broken somewhere, when there would be confusion. Their mastership, you know, like that between nations, is constantly changing. But there are always Napoleons who hold their own through many vicissitudes ; but the ordinary cow is continually liable to lose her foothold. Some cow she has always despised, and has often sent tossing across the yard at her horns' ends, some pleasant morning will return the compliment, and pay off old scores."

But my own observation has been that in herds in which there have been no important changes for several years, the question of might gets pretty well settled, and some one cow becomes the acknowledged ruler.

The bully of the yard is never the master, but usually a second or third rate pusher that never loses an opportunity to hook those beneath her, or to gore the masters if she can get them in a tight place. If such a one can get loose in the stable, she is quite certain to do mischief. She delights to pause in the open bars and turn and keep those at bay behind her till she sees a pair of threatening horns pressing towards her, when she quickly passes on. As one cow masters all, so there is one cow that is mastered by all. These are the two extremes of the herd, the head and the tail. Between them are all grades of authority, with none so poor but hath some poorer to do her reverence.

The cow has evidently come down to us from a wild or semi-wild state; perhaps is a descendant of those wild, shaggy cattle of which a small band is still preserved in some nobleman's park in Scotland. Cuvier seems to have been of this opinion. One of the ways in which her wild instincts still crop out is the disposition she shows in spring to hide her calf—a common practice among the wild herds. Her wild nature would be likely to come to the surface at this crisis if ever; and I have known cows that practised great secrecy in dropping their calves. As their time approached they grew restless, a wild and excited look was upon them, and if left free, they generally set out for the woods or for some other secluded spot. After the calf is several hours old, and has got upon its feet and had its first meal, the dam by some sign commands it to lie down and remain quiet while she goes forth to feed. If the calf is approached at such time it plays '"possum," assumes to be dead or asleep, till on finding this ruse does not succeed, it mounts to its feet, bleats loudly and fiercely, and charges desperately upon the intruder. But it recovers from this wild scare in a little while, and never shows signs of it again.

The habit of the cow, also, in eating the placenta, looks to me like a vestige of her former wild instincts—the instinct to remove everything that would give the wild beasts a clew or a scent, and so attract them to her helpless young.

How wise and sagacious the cows become that run upon the street, or pick their living along the highway. The mystery of gates and bars is at last solved to them. They ponder over them by night, they lurk about them by day, till they acquire a new sense till they become en *rapport* with them and know when they are open and unguarded. The garden gate, if it open into the highway at any point, is never out of the mind of these roadsters, or out of their calculations. They calculate upon the chances of its being left open a certain number of times in the season; and if it be but once, and only for five minutes, your cabbage and sweet corn suffer. What villager, or countryman either, has not been awakened at night by the squeaking and crunching of those piratical jaws under the window or in the direction of the vegetable patch? I have had the cows, after they had eaten up my garden, break into the stable where my own milcher was tied, and gore her and devour her meal. Yes, life presents but one absorbing problem to the street cow, and that is how to get into your garden. She catches glimpses of it over the fence or through the pickets, and her imagination or epigastrium is inflamed. When the spot is surrounded by a high board fence, I think I have seen her peeping at the cabbages through a knot-hole. At last she learns to open the gate. It is a great triumph of bovine wit. She does it with her horn or her nose, or may be with her ever ready tongue. I doubt if she has ever yet penetrated the mystery of the newer patent fastenings; but the old-fashioned thumb-latch she can see through, give her time enough.

A large, lank, muley or polled cow used to annoy me in this way when I was a dweller in a certain pastoral city. I more than half suspected she was turned in by some one; so one day I watched. Presently I heard the gate-latch rattle; the gate swung open, and in walked the old buffalo. On seeing me she turned and ran like a horse. I then fastened the gate on the inside and watched again. After long waiting the old cow came quickly round the corner and approached the gate. She lifted the latch with her nose. Then as the gate did not move, she lifted it again and again. Then she gently nudged it. Then, the obtuse gate not taking the hint, she butted it gently, then harder and still harder, till it rattled again. At this juncture I emerged from my hiding-place, when the old villain scampered off with great precipitation. She knew she was trespassing, and she had learned that there were usually some swift penalties attached to this pastime.

I have owned but three cows and loved but one. That was the first one, Chloe, a bright-red, curly-pated, golden-skinned Devonshire cow, that an ocean steamer landed for me upon the banks of the Potomac one bright May day many clover summers ago. She came from the north, from the pastoral regions of the Catskills, to graze upon the broad commons of the national capital. I was then the fortunate and happy lessee of an old place with an acre of ground attached, almost within the shadow of the dome of the Capitol. Behind a high but aged and decrepit board fence I indulged my rural and unclerical tastes. I could look up from my homely tasks and cast a potato almost in the midst of that cataract of marble steps that flows out of the north wing of the patriotic pile. Ah, when that creaking and sagging back gate closed behind me in the evening, I was happy; and when it opened for my egress thence in the morning, I was not happy. Inside that gate was a miniature farm redolent of homely, primitive life, a tumble-down house and stables and implements of agriculture and horticulture, broods of chickens, and growing pumpkins, and a thousand antidotes to the weariness of an artificial life. Outside of it were the marble and iron palaces, the paved and blistering streets, and the high, vacant mahogany desk of a government clerk. In that ancient enclosure I took an earth bath twice a day. I planted myself as deep in the soil as I could to restore the normal tone and freshness of my system, impaired by the above-mentioned government mahogany. I have found there is nothing like the earth to draw the various social distempers out of one. The blue devils take flight at once if they see you mean to bury them and make compost of them. Emerson intimates that the scholar had better not try to have two gardens; but I could never spend an hour hoeing up dock and red-root and twitch grass without in some way getting rid of many weeds and fungus, unwholesome growths that a petty, indoors life was for ever fostering in my own moral and intellectual nature.

But the finishing touch was not given till Chloe came. She was the jewel for which this homely setting waited. My agriculture had some object then. The old gate never opened with such alacrity as when she paused before it. How we waited for her coming! Should I send Drewer, the coloured patriarch, for her? No; the master of the house himself should receive Juno at the capital.

" One cask for you," said the clerk, referring to the steamer bill of lading.
"Then I hope it's a cask of milk," I said. " I expected a cow."
" One cask it says here."
"Well, let's see it; I'll warrant it has horns and is tied by a rope;" which proved to be the case, for there stood the only object that bore my name, chewing its cud, on the forward deck. How she liked the voyage I could not find out; but she seemed to relish so much the feeling of solid ground beneath her feet once more that she led me a lively step all the way home. She cut. capers in front of the White House, and tried twice to wind me up in the rope as we passed the Treasury. She kicked up her heels on the broad avenue and became very coltish as she came under the walls of the Capitol. But that night the long-vacant stall in the old stable was filled, and the next morning the coffee had met with a change of heart. I had to go out twice with the lantern and survey my treasure before I went to bed. Did she not come from the delectable mountains, and did I not have a sort of filial regard for her as toward my foster mother ?

This was during the Arcadian age at the capital, before the easy-going southern ways had gone out and the prim new northern ways had come in, and when the domestic animals were treated with distinguished consideration and granted the freedom of the city. There was a charm of cattle in the streets and upon the commons : goats cropped your rose-bushes through the pickets, and nooned upon your front porch, and pigs dreamed Arcadian dreams under your garden fence, or languidly frescoed it with pigments from the nearest pool. It was a time of peace; it was the poor man's golden age. Your cow, or your goat, or your pig led a vagrant, wandering life, and picked up a subsistence wherever they could, like the bees, which was almost everywhere. Your cow went forth in the morning and came home fraught with milk at night, and you never troubled yourself 'where she went or how far she roamed.

Chloe took very naturally to this kind of life. At first I had to go with her a few times and pilot her to the nearest commons, and then left her to her own wit, which never failed her. What adventures she had, what acquaintances she made, how far she wandered, I never knew. I never came across her in my walks or rambles. Indeed, on several occasions I thought I would look her up and see her feeding in national pastures, but I never could find her. There were plenty of cows, but they were all strangers. But punctually, between four and five o'clock in the afternoon, her white horns would be seen tossing above the gate and her impatient low be heard. Sometimes, when I turned her forth in the morning, she would pause and apparently consider which way she would go. Should she go toward Kendall Green to-day, or follow the Tiber, or over by the Big Spring, or out around Lincoln Hospital? She seldom reached a conclusion till she had stretched forth her neck and blown a blast on her trumpet that awoke the echoes in the very lantern on the dome of the Capitol. Then, after one or two licks, she would disappear around the-corner. Later in the season, when the grass was parched or poor on the commons, and the corn and cabbage tempting in the garden, Chloe was loath to depart in the morning, and her deliberations were longer than ever, and very often I had to aid her in coming to a decision.

For two summers she was a well-spring of pleasure and profit in my farm of one acre, when in an evil moment I resolved to part with her and try another. In an evil moment I say, for from that time my luck in cattle left me. The goddess never forgave me the execution of that rash and cruel resolve.

The day is indelibly stamped on my memory when I exposed my Chloe for sale in the public market-place. It was in November, a bright, dreamy, Indian summer day. A sadness oppressed me, not unmixed with guilt and remorse. An old Irish woman came to the market also with her pets to sell, a sow and five pigs, and took up a position next me. We condoled with each other; we bewailed the fate of our darlings together we berated in chorus the white-aproned but blood stained fraternity who prowled about us. When she went away for a moment I minded the pigs, and when I strolled about she minded my cow. How shy the innocent beast was of those carnal market-men ! How she would shrink away from them ! When they put out a hand to feel her condition she would "scrooch" down her back, or bend this way or that, as if the hand were a branding iron. So long as I stood by her head she felt safe—deluded creature—and chewed the cud of sweet content; but the moment I left her side she seemed filled with apprehension, and followed me with her eyes, lowing softly and entreatingly till I returned.

At last the money was counted out for her, and her rope surrendered to the hand of another. How that last look of alarm and incredulity, which I caught as I turned for a parting glance, went to my heart!

Her stall was soon filled, or partly filled, and this time with a native—a specimen of what may be called the corn-stalk breed of Virginia; a slender, furtive, long-geared heifer just verging on cowhood, that in spite of my best efforts would wear a pinched and hungry look. She evidently inherited a humped back. It was a family trait, and evidence of the purity of her blood. For the native-blooded cow of Virginia, from shivering over half rations of corn-stalks, in the open air during those bleak and windy winters, and roaming over those parched fields in summer, has come to have some marked features. For one thing, her pedal extremities seem lengthened; for another, her udder does not impede her travelling; for a third, her backbone inclines strongly to the curve ; then, she despiseth hay. This last is a sure test. Offer a thorough-bred Virginia cow hay, and she will laugh in your face; but rattle the husks or shucks, and she knows you to be her friend.

The new-comer even declined corn meal at first. She eyed it furtively, then sniffed it suspiciously, but finally discovered that it bore some relation to her native "shucks," when she fell to eagerly.

I cherish the memory of this cow, however, as the most affectionate brute I ever knew. Being deprived of her calf, she transferred her affections to her master, and would fain have made a calf of him, lowing in the most piteous and inconsolable manner when he was out of her sight, hardly forgetting her grief long enough to eat her meal, and entirely neglecting her beloved husks. Often in the middle of the night she would set up that sonorous lamentation, and continue it till sleep was chased from every eye in the household. This generally had the effect of bringing the object of her affection before her, but in a mood anything but filial or comforting. Still, at such times a kick seemed a comfort to her, and she would gladly have kissed the rod that was the instrument of my midnight wrath.

But her tender star was destined soon to a fatal eclipse. Being tied with too long a rope on one occasion during my temporary absence, she got her head into the meal-barrel, and stopped not till she had devoured nearly half a bushel of dry meal. The singularly placid and benevolent look that beamed from the meal-besmeared face when I discovered her was something to be remembered. For the first time also her spinal column came near assuming a horizontal line.

But the grist proved too much for her frail mill, and her demise took place on the third day, not of course without some attempt to relieve her on my part. I gave her, as is usual in such emergencies, everything I "could think of," and everything my neighbours could think of, besides some fearful prescriptions which I obtained from a German veterinary surgeon, but to no purpose. I imagined her poor maw distended and inflamed with the baking sodden mass which no physic could penetrate or enliven.

Thus ended my second venture in live stock. My third, which followed sharp upon the heels of this disaster, was scarcely more of a success. This time I led to the altar a buffalo cow, as they call the " muley" down South — a large, spotted, creamy-skinned cow, with a fine udder, that I persuaded a Jew drover to part with for ninety dollars. " Pag like a dish rack (rag)," said he, pointing to her udder after she had been milked. "You vill come pack and gif me the udder ten tollar " (for he had demanded an even hundred), he continued, "after you have had her a gouple of days." True, I felt like returning to him after a " gouple of days," but not to pay the other ten dollars. The cow proved to be as blind as a bat, though capable of counterfeiting the act of seeing to perfection. For did she not lift up her head and follow with her eyes a dog that scaled the fence and ran through the other end of the lot, and the next moment dash my hopes thus raised by trying to walk over a locust-tree thirty feet high? And when I set the bucket before her containing her first mess of meal, she missed it by several inches, and her nose brought up against the ground. Was it a kind of farsightedness and near blindness ? That was it, I think; she had genius, but not talent; she could see the man in the moon, but was quite oblivious to the man immediately in her front. Her eyes were telescopic, and required a long range.

As long as I kept her in the stall, or confined to the enclosure, this strange eclipse of her sight was of little consequence. But when spring came, and it was time for her to go forth and seek her livelihood in the city's waste places, I was embarrassed. Into what remote corners or into what terra incognita might she not wander? There was little doubt but she would drift around home in the course of the summer, or perhaps as often as every week or two; but could she be trusted to find her way back every night? Perhaps she could be taught. Perhaps her other senses were acute enough to in a measure compensate her for her defective vision. So I gave her lessons in the topography of the country. I led her forth to graze for a few hours each day and led her home again Then I left her to come home alone, which feat she accomplished very encouragingly. She came feeling her way along, stepping very high, but apparently a most diligent and interested sight-seer. But she was not sure of the right house when she got to it, though she stared at it very hard.

Again I turned her forth, and again she came back, her telescopic eyes apparently of some service to her. On the third day there was a fierce thunder-storm late in the afternoon, and old buffalo did not come home. It had evidently scattered and bewildered what little wit she had. Being barely able to navigate those streets on a calm day, what could she be expected to do in a tempest ?

After the storm had passed, and near sundown, I set out in quest of her, but could get no clew. I heard that two cows had been struck by lightning about a mile out on the commons. My conscience instantly told me that one of them was mine. It would be a fit closing of the third act of this pastoral drama. Thitherward I bent my steps, and there upon the smooth plain I beheld the scorched and swollen forms of two cows slain by thunderbolts, but neither of them had ever been mine.

The next day I continued the search, and the next, and the next. Finally I hoisted an umbrella over my head, for the weather had become hot, and set out deliberately and systematically to explore every foot of open common on Capitol Hill. I tramped many miles, and found every man's cow but my own—some twelve or fifteen hundred, I should think. I saw many vagrant boys and Irish and coloured women, nearly all of whom had seen a buffalo cow that very day that answered exactly to my description, but in such diverse and widely-separate places that I knew it was no cow of mine. And it was astonishing how many times I was myself deceived; how many rumps or heads, or line backs or white flanks I saw peeping over knolls or from behind fences or other objects that could belong to no cow but mine!

Finally I gave up the search, concluded the cow had been stolen, and advertised her, offering a reward. But days passed, and no tidings were obtained. Hope began to burn pretty low—was indeed on the point of going out altogether, when one afternoon, as I was strolling over the commons (for in my walks I still hovered about the scenes of my lost milcher, I saw the rump of a cow, over a grassy knoll, that looked familiar. Coming nearer, the beast lifted up her head; and, behold ! it was she ! only a few squares from home, where doubtless she had been most of the time. I had overshot the mark in my search. I had ransacked the far-off, and had neglected the near-at-hand, as we are so apt to do. But she was ruined as a milcher, and her history thenceforward was brief and touching !

BEFORE GENIUS.

Ifthere did not something else go to the making of literature besides mere literary parts, even the best of them, how long ago the old bards and Biblical writers would have been superseded by the learned professors and gentlemanly versifiers of later . times. Is there, to-day, a popular poet using the English language, who does not, in technical acquirements and in the artificial adjuncts of poetry—rhyme, metre, melody, and especially sweet, dainty fancies—surpass Europe's and Asia's loftiest and oldest ? Indeed, so marked is the success of the latter-day poets in this respect, that any ordinary reader may well be puzzled, and ask, if the shaggy old antique masters are poets, what are the refined and euphonious producers of our own day ?

If we were to inquire what this something else is, which is prerequisite to any deep and lasting success in literature, we should undoubtedly find that it is the man behind the book. It is the fashion of the day to attribute all splendid results to genius and culture. But genius and culture are not enough. "All other knowledge is hurtful to him who has not the science of honesty and goodness," says Montaigne. The quality of simple manhood, and the universal human traits, which form the bond of union between man and man, which form the basis of society, of the family, of government, of friendship, are quite overlooked; and the credit is given to some special facility, or brilliant and lucky hit. Does any one doubt that the great poets and artists are made up mainly of the most common universal human and heroic characteristics? that in them, though working to other ends, is all that construct the soldier, the sailor, the farmer, the discoverer, the bringer-to-pass in any field, and that their work is good and enduring in proportion as it is saturated and fertilised by the qualities of these? Good human stock is the main dependence. No great poet ever appeared except from a race of good fighters, good eaters, good sleepers, good breeders. Literature dies with the decay of the unliterary element. It is not in the spirit of something far away in the clouds or under the moon, something ethereal, visionary, and anti-mundane, that Angelo, Dante, and Shakespeare work, but in the spirit of the common nature, and the homeliest facts: through these, and not away from them, the path of the creator lies.

It is no doubt this tendency, always more or less marked in highly refined and cultivated times, to forget or overlook the primary basic qualities, and parade and make much of verbal and technical acquirements, that led Huxley to speak with such bitter scorn of the " senseless caterwauling of the literary classes," for this is not the only country in which books are produced that are a mere skin of elegant words blown up by copious literary gas.

In imaginative works especially, much depends upon the quality of mere weight. A stern, material inertia is indispensable. It is like the immobility and power of resistance of a piece of ordnance, upon which the force and efficacy of the projectile finally depend. In the most daring flights of the master, there is still something which remains indifferent and uncommitted, and which acts as reserve power, making the man always superior to his work. He must always leave the impression that if he wanted to pull harder or fly higher he could easily do so. In Homer there is much that is not directly available for Homer's purposes as poet. This is his personality—the real Homer which lies deeper than his talents and skill, and which works through these by indirections. This gives the authority; this is the unseen backer, which makes every promise good.

What depths can a man sound but his own, or what heights explore? "We carry within us," says Sir Thomas Browne, "the wonders we seek without us."

Indeed there is a strict moral or ethical dependence of the capacity to conceive or project great things upon the capacity to be or do them. It is as true as any law of hydraulics or statics, that the workmanship of a man can never rise above the level of his character. He can never adequately say or do anything greater than he himself is. There is no such thing, for instance, as deep insight into the mystery of Creation, without integrity and simplicity of character.

In the highest mental results and conditions the whole being sympathises. The perception of a certain range of truth, such as is indicated by Plato, Hegel, Swedenborg, and which is very far from what is called "religious " or "moral," I should regard as the best testimonial that could be offered of a man's probity and essential nobility of souL Is it possible to imagine a fickle, inconstant, or a sly, vain, mean person reading and appreciating Emerson? Think of the real men of science, the great geologists and astronomers, one opening up time, the other space! Shall mere intellectual acumen be accredited with these immense results? What noble pride, self-reliance, and continuity of character underlie Newton's deductions !

Only those books are for the making of men into which a man has gone in the making. Mere professional skill and sleight of hand, of themselves, are to be apprised as lightly in letters as in war or government, or any kind of leadership. Strong native qualities only avail in the long-run; and the more these dominate over the artificial endowments, sloughing or dropping the latter in the final result, the more we are refreshed and enlarged. Who has not, at some period of his life, been captivated by the rhetoric and fine style of nearly all the popular authors of the Arnold and Kingsley sort ? but, at last, waked up to discover that behind these brilliant names was no strong, loving man, but only a refined taste, a fertile invention, or a special talent of some kind or another.

Think of the lather of the modern novel, and the fashion-plate men and women that figure in them. What noble person has Dickens sketched, or has any novelist since Scott ? The utter poverty of almost every current novelist in any grand universal human traits in his own character, is shown in nothing more clearly than in the kind of interest the reader takes in his books. We are led along solely by the ingenuity of the plot, and a silly desire to see how the affair came out What must be the effect, long continued, of this class of jugglers working upon the sympathies and the imagination of a nation of gestating women ?

How the best modern novel collapses before the homely but immense human significance of Homer's celestial swine-herd entertaining divine Ulysses, or even the solitary watchman, in Æschylus' ***Agamemnon***, crouched, like a night-dog, on the roofs of the Atreidæ, waiting for the signal-fires that should announce the fall of sacred Ilion!

But one need not look long, even in contemporary British literature, to find a man. In the author of **Characteristics and Sartor Resartus** we surely encounter one of the true heroic cast. We are made aware that here is something more than a litterateur, something more than genius. Here is veracity, homely directness, and sincerity, and strong primary idiosyncracies. Here the man enters into the estimate of the author. There is no separating them, as there never is in great examples. A curious perversity runs through all, but in no way vitiates the result. In both his moral and intellectual natures Carlyle seems made with a sort of stub and twist, like the best gun-barrels. The knotty and corrugated character of his sentences suits well the peculiar and intense activity of his mind. What a transition from his terse and sharply-articulated pages, brimming with character and life, and a strange mixture of rage, humour, tenderness, poetry, philosophy, to the cold disbelief and municipal splendour of Macaulay 1 Nothing in Carlyle's contributions seems fortuitous. It all flows from a good and sufficient cause in the character of the man. Every great man is, in a certain way, an Atlas, with the weight of the world upon him. And if one is to criticise at all, he may say that if Carlyle had not been quite so conscious of this weight, his work would have been better done. Yet, to whom do we owe more, even as Americans? Antidemocratic in his opinions, he surely is not so in spirit, or in the quality of his make. The nobility of labour, and the essential nobility of man, were never so effectively preached before. The deadliest enemy of Democracy is not the warning or dissenting voice. But it is the spirit, rife among us, which would ensraft upon our hardy Western stock the sickly and decayed standards of the expiring feudal world.

With two or three exceptions, there is little as yet in American literature that shows much advance beyond the merely conventional and scholastic—little, I mean, in which one gets a whiff of the strong un-breathed air of mountain or prairie, or a taste of rude, new power that is like the tonic of the sea. Thoreau occupies a niche by himself. Thoreau was not a great personality; yet his writings have a strong characteristic flavour. He is anti-scorbutic, like leeks and onions. He has reference, also, to the highest truths.

It is very likely true that our most native and original characters do not yet take to literature. It is, perhaps, too early in the day. Iron and lime have to pass through the vegetable before they can reach the higher organisation of the animal, and may be this Western nerve and heartiness will yet emerge on the intellectual plane. Let us hope that it will indeed be Western nerve and heartiness when it gets there, and not Eastern wit and epigram !

In Abraham Lincoln we had a character of very marked and lofty type, the most suggestive study or sketch of the future American man that has yet appeared in our history. How broad, unconventional, and humane ! How democratic ! how adhesive ! No fine arabesque carvings, but strong, unhewn, native traits, and deep lines of care, toil, and human sympathy. Lincoln's Gettysburg speech is one of the most genuine and characteristic utterances in our annals. It has the true antique simplicity and im-pressiveness. It came straight from the man, and is as sure an index of character as the living voice, or the physiognomy, or the personal presence is. Indeed, it may be said of Mr. Lincoln's entire course while at the head of the nation, that no President, since the first, ever in his public acts allowed the man so fully to appear, or showed so little disposition to retreat behind the featureless political mask which seems to adhere to the idea of gubernatorial dignity.

It would hardly be fair to cite Everett's speech on the same occasion as a specimen of the opposite style, wherein ornate scholarship and the pride of talents dominate. Yet a stern critic would be obliged to say that, as an author, Everett allowed, for the most part, only the expurgated, complimenting, drawing-room man to speak ; and that, considering the need of America to be kept virile and broad at all hazards, his contribution, both as man and writer, falls immeasurably short of that of AbrahamLincoln.

What a noble specimen of its kind, and how free from any verbal tricks or admixture of literary sauce, is Thoreau's **Maine Woods**! And what a marked specimen of the opposite style is a certain other book I could mention in which these wild and grand scenes serve but as a medium to advertise the author's fund of classic lore.

Can there be any doubt about the traits and outward signs of a noble character, and is not the style of an author the manners of his soul ?

Is there a lyceum lecturer in the country who is above manoeuvring for the applause of his audience ? or a writer who is willing to make himself of no account for the sake of what he has to say? Even in the best there is something of the air and manners of a performer on exhibition. The newspaper, or magazine, or book, is a sort of raised platform, upon which the advertiser advances before a gaping and expectant crowd. Truly, how well he ***handles*** his subject! He turns it over, and around, and inside out, and top-side down. He tosses it about; he twirls it; he takes it apart and puts it together again, and knows well beforehand where the applause will come in. Any reader, in taking up the antique authors, must be struck by the contrast.

"In Æschylus," says Landor, "there is no trickery, no trifling, no delay, no exposition, no garrulity, no dogmatism, no declamation, no prosing, . . . but the loud clear challenge, the firm, unstealthy step of an erect, broad-breasted soldier."

On the whole the old authors are better than the new. The real question of literature is not simplified by culture or a multiplication of books, as the conditions of life are always the same, and are not made one whit easier by all the myriads of men and women who have lived upon the globe. The standing want is never for more skill, but for newer, fresher power—a more plentiful supply of arterial blood. The discoverer, or the historian, or the man of science, may begin where his predecessor left off, but the poet, or any artist, must go back for a fresh start. With him it is always the first day of creation, and he must begin at the stump or nowhere.

BEFOUR genius is manliness, and before beauty is power. The Russian novelist and poet, Turgeneiff, scattered all through whose works you will find unmistakable traits of greatness, makes one of his characters say, speaking of beauty, "The old masters—they never hunted after it; it comes of itself into their compositions, God knows whence, from heaven or elsewhere. The whole world belonged to them, but we are unable to clasp its broad spaces; our arms are too short."

From the same depth of insight come these lines from "Leaves of Grass," à propos of true poems :—

" They do not seek beauty—they are sought;
For ever touching them, or close upon them,
follows beauty, longing, fain, love-sick.".

The Roman was perhaps the first to separate beauty from use, and pursue it as ornament merely. He built his grand edifice —its piers, its vaults, its walls of brick and concrete—and then gave it a marble envelope copied from the Greek architecture. The latter could be stripped away, as in many cases it Was by the hand of time, and leave the essentials of the structure nearly complete. Not so with the Greek : he did not seek the beautiful; he was beauty; his building had no ornament, it was all structure ; in its beauty was the flower of necessity, the charm of inborn fitness and proportion. In other words, '' his art was structure refined into beautiful forms, not beautiful forms superimposed upon structure," as with the Roman. And it is in Greek mythology, is it not, that beauty is represented as riding upon the back of a lion ? as she assuredly always does in their poetry and art—rides upon power, or terror, or savage fate; not only rides upon, but is wedded and incorporated with: hence the athletic desire and refreshment her coming imparts.

This is the invariable order of Nature. Beauty without a rank material basis enfeebles. The world is not thus made; man is not thus begotten and nourished.

It comes to me there is something implied or understood when we look upon a beautiful object, that has quite as much to do with the impression made upon the mind as anything in the object itself; perhaps more. There is somehow an immense and undefined background of vast and unconscionable energy, as of earthquakes, and ocean storms, and cleft mountains; across which things of beauty play, and to which they constantly defer; and when this background is wanting, as it is in much current poetry, beauty sickens and dies, or at most has only a feeble existence.

Nature does nothing merely for beauty; beauty follows as the inevitable result; and the final impression of health and finish which her works make upon the mind is owing as much to these things which are not technically called beautiful, as to those which are. The former give identity to the latter. The one is to the other what substance is to form, or bone to flesh. The beauty of Nature includes all that is called beautiful as its flower; and all that is not called beautiful as its stalk and roots.

Indeed, when I go to the woods or fields, or ascend to the hill-top, I do not seem to be gazing upon beauty at all, but to be breathing it like the air. I am not dazzled or astonished; I am in no hurry to look, lest it be gone. I would not have the litter and débris removed, or the banks trimmed, or the ground painted. What I enjoy is commensurate with the earth and sky itself. It olings to the rocks and trees; it is kindred to the roughness and savagery ; it rises from every tangle and chasm; it perches on the dry oak-stubs with the hawks and buzzards; the crows shed it from their wings, and weave it into their nests of coarse sticks; the fox barks it, the cattle low it, and every mountain path leads to its haunts. I am not a spectator of, but a participator in it It is not an adornment; its roots strike to the centre of the earth.

All true beauty in Nature or in art is like the iridescent hue of mother-of-pearl, which is intrinsic and necessary, being the result of the arrangement of the particles—the flowering of the mechanism of the shell; or like the beauty of health which comes out of, and reaches back again to, the bones and the digestion. There is no grace like the grace of strength. What sheer muscular gripe and power lie back of the firm, delicate notes of the great violinist! "Wit," says Heine,—and the same thing is true of beauty, —"isolated, is worthless. It is only endurable when it rests on a solid basis."

In fact, beauty as a separate and distinct thing does not exist. Neither can it be reached by any sorting or sifting or clarifying process. It is an experience of the mind, and must be preceded by the conditions, just as light is an experience of the eye, and sound of the ear.

To attempt to manufacture beauty is as vain as to attempt to manufacture truth;

and to give it us in poems, or any form of art without a lion of some sort, a lion of truth, or fitness, or power, is to emasculate it and destroy its volition.

But current poetry is, for the most part, an attempt to do this very thing, to give us beauty without beauty's antecedents and foil. The poets want to spare us the annoyance of the beast. Since beauty is the chief attraction, why not have this part alone, pure and unadulterated—why not pluck the plumage from the bird, the flower from its stalk, the moss from the rock, the shell from the shore, the honey-bag from the bee, and thus have in brief what pleases us ? Hence, with rare exceptions, one feels on opening the latest book of poems like exclaiming, Well, here is the beautiful at last divested of everything else,—of truth, of power, of utility,—and one may add of beauty too. It charms as colour, or flowers, or jewels, or perfume, charms—and that is the end of it.

It is ever present to the true artist in his attempt to report Nature, that every object as it stands in the circuit of cause and effect has a history which involves its surroundings, and that the depth of the interest which it awakens in us is in proportion as its integrity in this respect is preserved. In Nature we are prepared for any opulence of colour, or vegetation, or freak of form, or display of any kind by its preponderance of the common, ever-present feature of the earth. The foil is always at hand. In like manner in the master poems we are never surfeited with mere beauty.

Woe to any artist who disengages beauty from the wide background of rudeness, darkness, and strength—and disengages her from absolute Nature ! The mild and beneficent aspects of Nature—what gulfs and abysses of power underlie them ! The great shaggy, barbaric earth, yet the summing up, the plenum of all we know or can know of beauty! So the orbic poems of the world have a foundation as of the earth itself, and are beautiful because they are something else first. Homer chose for his groundwork War, clinching, tearing, tugging war; in Dante, it is Hell; in Milton, Satan and the Fall; in Shakespeare, it is the fierce Feudal world, with its towering and kingly personalities ; in Byron, it is Revolt and diabolic passion. When we get to Tennyson the lion is a good deal tamed, but he is still there in the shape of the proud, haughty, and manly Norman, and in many forms yet stimulates the mind.

The perception of cosmical beauty comes by a vital original process. It is in some measure a creative act, and those works that rest upon it make demands—perhaps extraordinary ones—upon the reader or beholder. We regard mere surface glitter, or mere verbal sweetness, in a mood entirely passive, and with a pleasure entirely profitless. The beauty of excellent stage scenery seems much more obvious and easy of apprehension than the beauty of trees and hills themselves, inasmuch as the act of association in the mind is much easier and cheaper than the act of original perception.

Only the greatest works in any department afford any explanation of this wonder we call Nature, or aid the mind in arriving at correct notions concerning it. To copy here and there a line or a trait is no explanation; but to translate Nature into another language —to bridge it to us—to repeat, in some sort, the act of creation itself—is the final and crowning triumph of poetic art

II.

After the critic has enumerated all the stock qualities of the poet, as taste, fancy, melody, etc., it remains to be said that unless there is something in him that is ***living identity***, something analogous to the growing, pushing, reproducing forces of Nature, all the rest in the end pass for but little.

This is perhaps what the German critic, Lessing, really means by action, for true poems are more like deeds, expressive of something behind, more like acts of heroism. or devotion, or like personal character, than like thoughts, or intellections.

All the master poets have in their work an interior, chemical, assimilative property, a sort of gastric juice which dissolves thought and form, and holds in vital fusion religions, times, races, and the theory of their own construction, flaming up with electric and defiant power—power .without any admixture of resisting form, as in a living organism.

There are in Nature two types or forms, the cell and the crystal One means the organic, the other inorganic; one means growth, development, life; the other means reaction, solidification, rest. The hint and model of all creative works is the cell; critical, reflective, and philosophical works are nearer akin to the crystal; while there is much good literature that is neither the one nor the other distinctively, but which in a measure touches and includes both. But crystallic beauty, or cut and polished gems of thought, the result of the reflex rather than the direct action of the mind, we do not expect to find in the best poems, though they may be most prized by specially intellectual persons. In the immortal poems the solids are very few, or do not appear at all as solids—as lime and iron—any more than they do in organic nature, in the flesh of the peach or the apple. The main thing in every living organism is the vital fluids; seven-tenths of man is water; and seven-tenths of Shakespeare is passion, emotion—fluid humanity. Out of this arise his forms, as Venus arose out of the sea, and as man is daily built up out of the liquids of the body. We cannot taste, much less assimilate, a solid until it becomes a liquid; and your great idea, your sermon or moral, lies upon your poem a dead, cumbrous mass unless there is adequate heat and solvent, emotional power. Herein I think Wordsworth's " Excursion " fails as a poem. It has too much solid matter. It. is an over-freighted bark that does not ride the waves buoyantly and lifelike; far less so than Tennyson's "In Memoriam," which is just as truly a philosophical poem as the " Excursion." (Wordsworth is the fresher poet; his poems seem really to have been written in the open air, and to have been brought directly under the oxygenating influence of outdoor nature; while in Tennyson this influence seems tempered or further removed.)

The physical cosmos itself is not a thought, but an act. Natural objects do not affect us like well wrought specimens or finished handicraft, which have nothing to follow, but as living, procreating energy. Nature is perpetual transition. Everything passes and presses on; there is no pause, no completion, no explanation. To produce and multiply endlessly, without ever reaching the last possibility of excellence, and without committing herself to any end, is the law of Nature.

These considerations bring us very near the essential difference between prose and poetry, or rather between the poetic and the didactic treatment of a subject.

The essence of creative art is always the same; namely, interior movement and fusion; while the method of the didactic or prosaic treatment is fixity, limitation. The latter must formulate and define; but the principle of the former is to flow, to suffuse, to mount, to escape. We can conceive of life only as something constantly ***becoming***. It plays for ever on the verge. It is never in loco, but always in transitu. Arrest the wind, and it is no longer the wind; close your hands upon the light, and behold, it is gone.

The antithesis of art in method is science, as Coleridge has intimated. As the latter aims at the particular, so the former aims at the universal. One would have truth of detail, the other truth of ensemble. The method of science may be symbolised by the straight line, that of art by the curve. The results of science, relatively to its aim, must be parts and pieces; while art must give the whole in every act; not quanti-tively of course, but qualitively by the integrity of the spirit in which it works.

The Greek mind will always be the type of the artist mind, mainly because of its practical bent, its healthful objectivity. The Greek never looked inward, but outward. Criticism and speculation were foreign to him. His head shows a very marked predominance of the motor and perceptive principle over the reflective. The expression of the face is never what we call intellectual or thoughtful, but commanding. His gods are not philosophers, but delight in deeds, justice, rulership

Among the differences between the modern and the classical aesthetic mind is the greater precision and definiteness of the latter. The modern genius is Gothic, and demands in art a certain vagueness and spirituality like that of music, refusing to be grasped and formulated. Hence, for us (and this is undoubtedly an improvement) there must always be something about a poem, or any work of art, besides the evident intellect or plot of it, or what is on its surface, or what it tells. This something is the Invisible, the Undefined, almost Unexpressed, and is perhaps the best part of any work of art, as it is of a noble Personality. To amuse, to exhibit culture, to formulate the aesthetic, or even to excite the emotions, is by no means all—is not even the deepest part. Beside these, and enclosing all, is the I general impalpable effect, like a good air, or the subtle presence of good spirits, word- J less, but more potent far than words. As in 1 the superbest person, it is not merely what I he or she says, or knows, or shows, or even [how they behave, but in the silent qualities I like gravitation that insensibly but resist- 1 lessly hold us; so in a good poem, or any other expression of art.

EMERSON.
I.

WHEREIN the race has so far lost and gained in being transplanted from Europe to the New England soil and climate, is well illustrated by the writings of Emerson. There is greater refinement and sublimation of thought, greater clearness and sharpness of outline, greater audacity of statement, but, on the other hand, there is a loss of bulk, of unction, of adipose tissue, and shall we say of power ?

Emerson is undoubtedly a master on the New England scale—such a master as the land and race are capable of producing. He stands out clear and undeniable. The national type, as illustrated by that section of the country, is the purest and strongest in him of any yet. He can never suffer eclipse. Compared with the English or German master, he is undoubtedly deficient in viscera, in moral and intellectual stomach; but, on the other hand, he is of a fibre and quality hard to match in any age or land. From first to last he strikes one as something extremely pure and compact, like a nut or an egg. Great matters and tendencies lie folded in him, or rather are summarised in his pages. He writes short but pregnant chapters on great themes, as in his English Traits, a book like rich preserves put up pound for pound, a pound of Emerson to every pound of John Bull. His chapter on Swedenborg in Representative Men is a good sample of his power to abbreviate and restate with added force. His mind acts like a sun-lens in gathering the cold pale beams of that luminary to a focus which warms and stimulates the reader in a surprising manner. The gist of the whole matter is here; and how much weariness and dulness and plodding is left out!

In fact, Emerson is an essence, a condensation; more so, perhaps, than any other man who has appeared in literature. Nowhere else is there such a preponderance of pure statement, of the very attar of thought over the bulkier, circumstantial, qualifying, or secondary elements. He gives us net results. He is like those strong artificial fertilisers. A pinch of him is equivalent to a page or two of Johnson, and he is pitched many degrees higher as an essayist than even Bacon. He has had an immediate stimulating effect upon all the best minds of the country ; how deep or lasting this influence will be remains to be seen.

This point and brevity has its convenience and value especially in certain fields of literature. I by no means would wish to water Emerson ; yet it will not do to lose sight of the fact that mass and inertia are indispensable to the creator. Considering him as Poet alone, I have no doubt of his irremediable deficiency here. You cannot have broad, massive effect, deep lights and shade, or a torrent of power, with such extreme refinement and condensation. The superphosphates cannot take the place of the coarser, bulkier fertilisers. Especially in poetry do we require pure thought to be well diluted with the human, emotional qualities. In the writing most precious to the race, how little is definition and intellectual formula, and how much is impulse, emotion, will-character, blood, chyle, etc. We must have liquids and gases and solvents. We perhaps get more of them in Carlyle. Emerson's page has more serene astral beauty than Carlyle's, but not that intense blast-furnace heat that melts down the most obdurate facts and characters into something plastic and poetical. Emerson's ideal is always the scholar, the man of books and ready wit; Carlyle's hero is a riding or striding ruler, or a master worker in some active field.

The antique mind no doubt affords the true type of health and wholeness in this respect. The Greek could see, and feel, and paint, and carve, and speak, nothing but emotional man. In Nature he saw nothing but personality — nothing but human or superhuman qualities ; to him the elements all took the human shape. Of that vague, spiritual, abstract something which we call Nature he had no conception. He had no sentiment, properly speaking, but impulse and will-power. And the master minds of the world, in proportion to their strength, their spinal strength, have approximated to this type. Dante, Angelo, Shakespeare, Byron, Goethe saw mainly man, and him not abstractly, but concretely. And this is the charm of Burns and the glory of Scott. Carlyle has written the best histories and biographies of modern times, because he sees man with such fierce and steadfast eyes. Emerson sees him also, but he is not interested in him as a man, but mainly as a spirit, as a demigod, or as a wit or philosopher.

Emerson's quality has changed a good deal in his later writings. His corn is no longer in the milk; it has grown hard, and we that read have grown hard too. He has now ceased to be an expansive, revolutionary force, but he has not ceased to be a writer of extraordinary gripe and unexpected resources of statement. His startling piece of advice, "Hitch your wagon to a star," is typical of the man, as combining the most unlike and widely separate qualities. Because, not less marked than his idealism and mysticism is his shrewd common-sense, his practical bent, his definite-ness in fact, the sharp New England mould in which he is cast. He is the master Yankee, the centennial flower of that thrifty and peculiar stock. More especially in his later writings and speakings do we see the native New England traits—the alertness, eagerness, inquisitiveness, thrift, dryness, archness, caution, the nervous energy as distinguished from the old English unction and vascular force. How he husbands himself what prudence, what economy, always spending up, as he says, and not down ! How alert, how attentive; what an inquisitor; always ready with some test question, with some fact or idea to match or verify, ever on the lookout for some choice bit of adventure . or information, or some anecdote that has pith and point.! No tyro basks and takes his ease in his presence, but is instantly put on trial and must answer or be disgraced. He strikes at an idea like a falcon at a bird. His great fear seems to be lest there be some fact or point worth knowing that will escape him. He is a close-browed miser of the scholar's gains. He turns all values into intellectual coin. Every book or person or experience is an investment that will or will not warrant a good return in ideas. He goes to the Radical Club, or to the literary gathering, and listens with the closest attention to every word that is said in hope that something will be said, some word dropped, that has the ring of the true metal. Apparently he does not permit himself a moment's indifference or inattention. His own pride is always to have the ready change, to speak the exact and proper word, to give to every occasion the dignity of wise speech. You are bartered with for your best. There is no profit in life but in the interchange of ideas, and the chief success is to have a head well filled with them. Hard cash at that; no paper promises satisfy him; he loves the clink and glint of the real coin.

His earlier writings were more flowing and suggestive, and had reference to larger problems; but now everything has got weighed and stamped and converted into the medium of wise and scholarly conversation. It is of great value; these later essays are so many bags of genuine coin, which it has taken a lifetime to hoard; not all gold, but all good, and the fruit of wise industry and economy.

I know of no other writing that yields the reader so many strongly-stamped medallion-like sayings and distinctions. There is a perpetual refining and recoining of the current wisdom of life and conversation. It is the old gold or silver or copper, but how bright and new it looks in his pages! Emerson loves facts, things, objects, as the workman his tools. He makes everything serve. The stress of expression is so great that he bends the most obdurate element to his purpose; as the bird, under her keen necessity, weaves the most contrary and diverse materials into her nest. He seems to like best material that is a little refractory; it makes his page more piquant and stimulating. Within certain limits he loves roughness, but not to the expense of harmony. He has a wonderful hardiness and push. Where else in literature is there a mind, moving in so rare a medium, that gives one such a sense of tangible resistance and force ? It is a principle in mechanics that velocity is twice as great as mass: double your speed, and you double your heat though you halve your weight. In like manner this body we are considering is not the largest, but its speed is great, and the intensity of its impact with objects and experience is almost without parallel Everything about a man like Emerson is important. I find his phrenology and physiognomy more than ordinarily typical and suggestive. Look at his picture there large strong features on a small face and head no blank spaces ; all given up to expression ; a high predaoeous nose, a sinewy brow, a massive, benevolent chin. In most men there is more face than feature, but here is a vast deal more feature than face, and a corresponding alertness and emphasis of character. Indeed, the man is made after this fashion. He is all type; his expression is transcendent. His mind has the hand's pronounced anatomy, its cords and sinews and multiform articulations and processes, its opposing and coordinating power. If his brain is small, its texture is fine, and its convolutions deep. There have been broader and more catholic natures, but few so towering and audacious in expression and so rich in characteristic traits. Every scrap and shred of him is important and related. Like the strongly aromatic herbs and simples, sage, mint, wintergreen, sassafras, the least part carries the flavour of the whole. Is there one indifferent, or equivocal or unsympathising drop of blood in him ? Where he is at all he is entirely—nothing extemporaneous ; his most casual word seems to have laid in pickle a long time, and is saturated through and through with the Emersonian brine. Indeed, so pungent and penetrating is his quality, that even his quotations seem more than half his own.

He is a man who occupies every inch of his rightful territory ; he is there in proper person to the furthest bound. Not every man is himself and his best self at all times, and to his finger points. Many great characters, perhaps the greatest, have more or less neutral or waste ground. You must penetrate a distance before you reach the real quick. Or there is a good wide margin of the commonplace which is sure to put them on good terms with the mass of their fellow-citizens. And one would think Emerson could afford to relax a little; that he had earned the right to a dull page or two now and then. The second best or third best word sometimes would make us appreciate his first best all the more. Even his godfather Plato nods occasionally, but Emerson's good breeding will not for a moment permit such a slight to the reader.

Emerson's peculiar quality is very subtle, but very sharp, and firm, and unmistakable. It is not analogous to the commoner, slower-going elements, as heat, air, fire, water, etc., but is nearer akin to that elusive but potent something we call electricity. It is abrupt, freaky, unexpected, and always communicates a little wholesome shock. It darts this way and that, and connects the far and the near in every line. There is always a leaping thread of light, and there is always a kind of answering peal or percussion. With what quickness and suddenness extremes are brought together ! The reader is never prepared for what is to come next; the spark will most likely leap from some source or fact least thought of. His page seldom glows and burns, but there is a never-ceasing crackling and discharge of moral and intellectual force into the mind.

His chief weapon, and one that he never lays down, is identical with that of the great wits; namely, surprise. The point of his remark or idea is always sprung upon the reader, never quietly laid before him. He has a mortal dread of tameness and flatness, and would make the very water we drink bite the tongue.

He has been from the first a speaker and lecturer, and his style has been largely modelled according to the demand of those sharp, heady New England audiences for ceaseless intellectual friction and chafing. Hence every sentence is braided hard, and more or less knotted, and though of silk, makes the mind tingle. He startles by overstatement, by understatement, by paradox, by antithesis, and by synthesis. Into every sentence enters the unexpected the congruous leaping from the incongruous, the high coming down, the low springing up, likeness, relation suddenly coming into view where before was only difference or antagonism. How he delights to bring the reader up with a short turn, to impale him on a knotty point, to explode one of his verbal bomb-shells under his very nose! Yet there is no trickery or rhetorical legerdemain. His heroic fibre always saves him.

The language in which Taine describes Bacon applies with even more force to Emerson:

" Bacon' he says, "is a producer of conceptions and of sentences. The matter being explored, he says to us :Such it is ; touch it not on that side ; it must be approached from the other.' Nothing more; no proof, no effort to convince; he affirms, and nothing more; he has thought in the manner of artists and poets, and he speaks after the manner of prophets and seers. 'Cogita el visa' this title of one of his books might be the title of all. His process is that of the creators; it is intuition, not reasoning. . . . There is nothing more hazardous, more like fantasy, than this mode of thought when it is not checked by natural and good strong common-sense. This common-sense, . which is a kind of natural divination, the stable equilibrium of an intellect always gravitating to the true, like the needle to the north pole, Bacon possesses in the highest degree. He has a pre-eminently practical, even an utilitarian mind."

It is significant, and is indeed the hidden seed or root, out of which comes the explanation of much, if not the main part of his life and writings, that Emerson comes of a long line of clergymen; that the blood in his veins has been teaching, and preaching, and thinking and growing austere, these many generations. One wonders that it is still so bounding and strong, so red with iron and quick with oxygen. But in him seems to be illustrated one of those rare cases in the genealogy of families where the best is carried forward each time and steadily recruited and intensified. It does not seem possible for any man to become just what Emerson is from the stump, though perhaps great men have been the fruit of one generation ; but there is a quality in him, an aroma of fine manners, a propriety, a chivalry in the blood that dates back, and has been refined and transmitted many times. Power is born with a man, and is always first hand, but culture, genius, noble instincts, gentle manners, etc., or the easy capacity for these things, may be, and to a greater or lesser extent are, the contribution of the past. Emerson's culture is radical and ante-natal, and never fails him. The virtues of all those New England ministers and all those tomes of sermons are in this casket. One fears sometimes that he has been too much clarified, or that there is not enough savage grace or original viciousness and grit in him to save him. How he hates the roysterers, and all the rank, turbulent, human passions, and is chilled by the thought that perhaps after all Shakespeare led a vulgar life !

When Tyndall was here he showed us how the dark, coarse, invisible heat rays could be strained out of the spectrum; or in other words, that every solar beam was weighed with a vast, nether, invisible side, which made it a lever of tremendous power in organic nature. After some such analogy one sees how the highest order of power in the intellectual world draws upon and is nourished by those rude, primitive, barbaric human qualities that our culture and pietism tend to cut off and strain out. Our culture has its eye on the other end of the spectrum, where the fine violet and indigo rays are; but all the lifting, rounding, fructifying powers of the system are in the coarse, dark rays—the black devil—at the base. The angel of light is yoked with the demon of darkness, and the pair create and sustain the world.

In rare souls like Emerson, the fruit of extreme culture, it is inevitable that atleast some of the heat rays should be lost, and we miss them especially when we contrast him with the elder masters. The elder masters did not seem to get rid of the coarse or vulgar in human life, but royally accepted it, and struck their roots into it, and drew from it sustenance and power; but there is an ever-present suspicion that Emerson prefers the saints to the sinners; prefers the prophets and seers to Homer, Shakespeare, and Dante. Indeed it is to be distinctly stated and emphasised that Emerson is essentially a priest, and that the key to all he has said and written is to be found in the fact that his point of view is not that of the acceptor, the creator Shakespeare's point of view but that of the refiner and selector the priests' point of view. He described his own state rather than that of mankind when he said, " The human mind stands ever in perplexity, demanding intellect, demanding sanctity, impatient equally of each without the other."

Much surprise has been expressed in literary circles in this country that Emerson has not followed up his first off-hand indorsement of Walt Whitman with fuller and more deliberate approval of that poet, but has rather taken the opposite tack. But the wonder is that he should have been carried off his feet at all in the manner he was; and it must have been no ordinary breeze that did it. Emerson shares with his contemporaries the vast preponderance of the critical and discerning intellect over the fervid, manly qualities and faith. His power of statement is enormous; his scope of being is not enormous. The prayer he uttered many years ago for a poet of the modern, one who could see in the gigantic materialism of the times the carnival of the same deities we so much admire in Greece and Rome, etc., seems to many to have even been explicitly answered in Whitman; but Emerson is balked by the cloud of materials, the din and dust of action, and the moving armies, in which the god comes enveloped.

But Emerson has his difficulties with all the poets. Homer is too literal, Milton too literary, and there is too much of the whooping savage in Whitman. He seems to think the real poet is yet to appear; a poet on new terms, the reconciler, the poet-priest one who shall unite the whiteness and purity of the saint with the power and unction of the sinner; one who shall bridge the chasm between Shakespeare and St. John. For when our Emerson gets on his highest horse, which he does only on two or three occasions, he finds Shakespeare only a half man, and that it would take Plato and Menu and Moses and Jesus to complete him. Shakespeare, he says, rested with the symbol, with the festal beauty of the world, and did not take the final step, and explore the essence of things, and ask, "Whence? What and Whither ? " He was not wise for himself; he did not lead a beautiful, saintly life, but ate, and drank, and revelled, and affiliated with all manner of persons, and quaffed the cup of life with gusto and relish. The elect, spotless souls will always look upon the heat and unconscious optimism of the great poet with deep regret. But if man would not become emasculated, if human life is to continue, we must cherish the coarse as well as the fine, the root as well as the top and flower. The poet-priest in the Emersonian sense has never yet appeared, and what reason have we to expect him? The poet means life, the whole of life all your ethics and philosophies, and essences and reason of things, in vital play and fusion, clothed with form and colour, and throbbing with passion; the priest means a part, a thought, a precept; he means suppression, expurgation, death. To have gone further than Shakespeare would have been to cease to be a poet, and become a mystic or seer.

Yet it would be absurd to say, as a leading British literary journal recently did, that Emerson is not a poet. He is one kind of a poet. He has written plenty of poems that are as melodious as the hum of a wild bee in the air chords of wild æolian music.

Undoubtedly his is, on the whole, a bloodless kind of poetry.' It suggests the pale grey matter of the cerebrum rather than flesh and blood. Mr. Wm. Rossetti has made a suggestive remark about him. He is not so essentially a poet, says this critic, as he is a Druid that wanders among the bards, and strikes the harp with even more than bardic stress.

Not in the poetry of any of his contemporaries is there such a burden of the mystery of things or such round wind-harp tones, lines so tense and resonant, and blown upon by a breeze from the highest heaven of thought. In certain respects he has gone beyond any other. He has gone beyond the symbol to the thing signified. He has emptied poetic forms of their meaning, and made poetry of that. He would fain cut the world up into stars to shine in the intellectual firmament. He is more and he is less than the best.

He stands among other poets like a pine-tree amid a forest of oak and maple. He seems to belong to another race, and to other climes and conditions. He is great in one direction, up; no dancing leaves, but rapt needles; never abandonment, never a tossing and careering, never an avalanche of emotion; the same in sun and snow, scattering his cones, and with night and obscurity amid his branches. He is moral first and last, and it is through his impassioned and poetic treatment of the moral law that he gains such an ascendency over his reader. He says, as for other things he makes poetry of them, but the moral law makes poetry of him. He sees in the world only the ethical, but he sees it through the aesthetic faculty. Hence his page has the double charm of the beautiful and the good.

II.

One of the penalties Emerson pays for his sharp decision, his mental pertinence and resistance, is the curtailment of his field of vision and enjoyment He is one of those men whom the gods drive with blinders on, so that they see fiercely in only a few directions. Supreme lover as he is of poetry,— Herrick's poetry,—yet from the whole domain of what may be called emotional poetry, the poetry of fluid humanity, tallied by music, he seems to be shut out. This may be seen by his reference to Shelley in his last book, ***Letters and Social Aims*** and by his preference of the metaphysical poet throughout his writings. Wordsworth's famous "Ode" is, he says, the high-water mark of English literature. What he seems to value most in Shakespeare is the marvellous wit, the pregnant sayings. He finds no poet in France, and in his ***English Traits*** credits Tennyson with little but melody and colour. (In our last readings, do we not surely come to feel the manly and robust fibre beneath Tennyson's silken vestments ?) He demands of poetry that it be a kind of spiritual manna, and is at last forced to confess that there are no poets, and that when such angels do appear, Homer and Milton will be tin pans.

One feels that this will not do, and that health, and wholeness, and the wellbeing of man, are more in the keeping of Shakespeare than in the hands of Zoroaster or any of the saints. I doubt if that rarefied air will make good red blood, and plenty of it

But Emerson makes his point plain, and is not indebted to any of his teachers for it. It is the burden of all he writes upon the subject. The long discourse that opens his last volume has numerous sub-headings— as "Poetry," "Imagination," "Creation," " Morals," and " Transcendency;" but it is all a plea for transcendency. I am reminded of the story of an old Indian chief who was invited to some great dinner where the first course was "succotash." When the second course was ready the old Indian said he would have a little more succotash, and when the third was ready he called for more succotash, and so with the fourth and fifth, and on to the end. In like manner Emerson will have nothing but the "spiritual law" in poetry, and he has an enormous appetite for that. Let him have it, but why should he be so sure that mankind all want succo tash ? Mankind finally comes to care little for what any poet has Jo say, .but only for what he has to sing. We want the pearl of thought dissolved in the wine of life. How much better are sound bones and a good digestion in poetry than all the philosophy and transcendentalism in the world !

What one comes at last to want is power, mastery; and whether it be mastery over the subtleties of the intellect as in Emerson himself, or over the passions and the springs of action, as in Shakespeare, or over our terrors and the awful hobgoblins of hell and Satan, as in Dante, or over vast masses and spaces of Nature and the abysms of aboriginal man, as in Walt Whitman—what matters it ? Are we not refreshed by all ? There is one mastery in Burns, another in Byron, another in Rabelais, and in Victor Hugo, and in Tennyson, and though the critic has his preferences, though he affect one more than another, yet who shall say this one is a poet and that one is not? "There may be any number of supremes," says the master, and " one by no means contravenes another." Every gas is a vacuum to every other gas, says Emerson, quoting the scientist; and every great poet complements and leaves the world free to every other great poet.

Emerson's limitation or fixity is seen also in the fact that he has taken no new step in his own direction, if indeed another step could be taken in that direction, and not step off. He is a prisoner on his peak. He cannot get away from the old themes. His later essays are upon essentially the same subjects as his first. He began by writing upon nature, greatness, manners, art, poetry, etc., and he is still writing upon them. He is a husbandman who practises no rotation of crops, but submits to the exhaustive process of taking about the same things from his soil year after year. Some readers think they detect a falling off. It is evident there is not the same spontaneity, and that the soil has to be more and more stirred and encouraged, which is not at all to be wondered at.

But if Emerson has not advanced, he has not receded, at least in conviction and will, which is always the great danger with our bold prophets. The world in which he lives, the themes upon which he writes, never become hackneyed to him. They are always fresh and new. He has hardened, but time has not abated one jot or tittle his courage and hope no cynicism and no relaxing of his hold, no decay of his faith, while the nobleness of his tone, the chivalry of his utterance, is even more marked than at first. Better a hundred-fold than his praise of fine manners is the delicacy and courtesy and the grace of generous breeding displayed on every page. Why does one grow impatient and vicious when Emerson writes of fine manners, and the punctilios of conventional life, and feel like kicking into the street every divinity enshrined in the drawing-room? It is a kind of insult to a man to speak the word in his presence. Purify the parlours indeed, by keeping out the Choc-taws, the laughers! Let us go and hold high carnival for a week, and split the ears of the groundlings with our "contemptible squeals of joy." And when he makes a dead set at praising eloquence I find myself instantly on the side of the old clergyman he tells of who prayed that he might never be eloquent; or when he makes the test of a man an intellectual one, as his skill at repartee, and praises the literary crack shot, and defines manliness to be readiness, as he does in this last volume, and in the preceding one, I am filled with a perverse envy of all the confused and stammering heroes of history. Is Washington faltering out a few broken and ungrammatical sentences, in reply to the vote of thanks of the Virginia legislature, less manly than the glib tongue in the court-room or in the club that can hit the mark every time ? The test of a wit or -of a scholar is one thing; the test of a man, I take it, is quite another. In this and some other respects Emerson is well antidoted by Carlyle, who lays the stress on the opposite qualities, and charges his hero to hold his tongue. But one cheerfully forgives Emerson the way he puts his thumb-nail on the bores. He speaks feelingly, and no doubt from as deep an experience as any man in America.

I really hold Emerson in such high esteem, that I think I can safely indulge myself in a little more fault-finding with him.

I think it must be admitted that he is deficient in sympathy. This accounts in a measure for his coolness, his self-possession, and that kind of uncompromising rectitude or inflexibleness that marks his career, and that he so lauds in his essays. No man is so little liable to be warped or compromised in any way as the unsympathetic man. Emerson's ideal is the man who stands firm, who is unmoved, who never laughs, or apologises, or deprecates, or makes concessions, or assents through good-nature, or goes abroad; who is not afraid of giving offence; " who answers you without supplication in his eye "—in fact, who stands like a granite pillar amid the slough of life. You may wrestle with this man, he says, or swim with him, or lodge in the same chamber with him, or eat at the same table, and yet he is a thousand miles off, and can at any moment finish with you. He is a sheer precipice, is this man, and not to be trifled with. You shrinking, quivering, acquiescing natures, avaunt! You sensitive plants, you hesitating, indefinite creatures, you uncertain around the edges, you non-resisting, and you heroes, whose courage is quick, but whose wit is tardy, make way, and let the human crustacean pass. Emerson is moulded upon this pattern. It is no mush and milk that you get at this table. "A great man is coming to dine with me; I do not wish to please him; I wish that he should wish to please me." On the lecture stand he might be of wood so far as he is responsive to the moods and feelings of his auditors. They must come to him; he will not go to them; but they do not always come. Latterly the people have felt insulted, the lecturer showed them so little respect. Then, before a promiscuous gathering, and in stirring and eventful times like ours, what anachronisms most of his lectures are, even if we take the high ground that they are pearls before swine. The swine may safely demand some apology of him who offers them pearls instead of corn. Emerson's fibre is too fine for large public uses. He is what he is, and is to be accepted as such, only let us ***know*** what he is. He does not speak to universal conditions, or to human nature in its broadest, deepest, strongest phases. His thought is far above the great sea-level of humanity, where stand most of the world's masters. He is like one of those marvellously clear mountain lakes whose water-line runs above all the salt seas of the globe. He is very precious, taken at his real worth. Why find fault with the isolation and the remoteness in view of the sky-like purity and depth ?

Still I must go on sounding and exploring him, reporting where I touch bottom, and where I do not. He reaps great advantage from his want of sympathy. The world makes no inroads upon him through this channel. He is not distracted by the throng or may be the mob of emotions that find entrance here. He shines like a star un-dimmed by current events. He speaks as from out the interstellar spaces. 'Tis vulgar sympathy makes mortals of us all, and I think Emerson's poetry finally lacks just that human colouring and tone, that flesh tint of the heart, that vulgar sympathy with human life as such imparts.

But after we have made all possible deductions from Emerson, there remains the fact that he is a living force, and, tried by home standards, a master. Wherein does the secret of his power lie ? He is the prophet and philosopher of young men. The old man and the man of the world make little of him, but of the youth who is ripe for him he takes almost an unfair advantage. One secret of his charm I take to be the instant success with which he transfers our interest in the romantic, the chivalrous, the heroic, to the sphere of morals and the intellect. We are let into another realm unlooked for, where daring and imagination also lead. The secret and suppressed heart finds a champion. To the young man fed upon the penny precepts and staple John-sonianism of English literature, and of what is generally doled out in the schools and colleges, it is a surprise; it is a revelation. A new world opens before him. The nebulae of his spirit are resolved or shown to be irresolvable. The fixed stars of his inner firmament are brought immeasurably near. He drops all other books. He will gaze and wonder. From Locke or Johnson or Wayland to Emerson is like a change from the school history to the **Arabian Nights**, There may be extravagances and some jugglery, but for all that the lesson is a genuine one, and to us of this generation immense.

Emerson is the knight errant of the moral sentiment. He leads, in our time and country, one illustrious division, at least, in the holy crusade of the affections and the intuitions against the usurpations of tradition and theological dogma. He marks the flower, the culmination, under American conditions and in the finer air of the new world, of the reaction begun by the German philosophers, and passed along by later French and English thinkers, of man against circumstance, of spirit against form, of the present against the past. What splendid affirmation, what inspiring audacity, what glorious egoism, what generous brag, what sacred impiety ! There is an éclat about his words, and a brave challenging of immense odds that is like an army with banners. It stirs the blood like a bugle call: beauty, bravery, and a sacred cause — the three things that win with us always. The first essay is a forlorn hope. See what the chances are: "The world exists for the education of each man, . . . He should see that he can live all history in his own person. He must sit solidly at home, and not suffer himself to be bullied by kings or empires, but know that he is greater than all the geography and all the government of the world; he must transfer the point of view from which history is commonly read from Rome and Athens and London to himself, and not deny his conviction that he is the court, and if England or Egypt have anything to say to him, he will try the case; if not, let them for ever be silent." In every essay that follows there are the same great odds, and the same electric call to the youth to face them. It is indeed as much a world of fable and romance that Emerson introduces us to as we get in Homer or Herodotus. It is true. all true—true as Arthur and his knights, or **Pilgrim's Progress**, and I pity the man who has not tasted its intoxication, or who can see nothing in it.

The intuitions are the bright band, without armour or shield, that slay the mailed and bucklered giants of the understanding. Government, institutions, religions, fall before the glance of the hero's eye. Art and literature, Shakespeare, Angelo, Æschylus, are humble suppliants before you, the king. The commonest fact is idealised, and the whole relation of man to the universe is thrown into a kind of gigantic perspective. It is not much to say there is exaggeration; the very start makes Mohammed's attitude toward the mountain tame. The mountain shall come to Mohammed, and in the eyes of all horn readers of Emerson the mountain does come, and comes with alacrity.

Some shrewd judges apprehend that Emerson is not going to last; basing their opinion npon the fact, already alluded to, that we outgrow him, or pass through him as through an experience that we cannot repeat. He is but a bridge to other things ; he gets you over. He is an exceptional fact in literature, say they, and does not represent lasting or universal conditions. He is too fine for the rough wear and tear of ages. True, we do not outgrow Dante, or Cervantes, or Bacon; and I doubt if the Anglo-Saxon stock at least ever outgrows that king of romancers, Walter Scott. These men and their like appeal to a larger audience, and in some respects a more adult one; at least one more likely to be found in every age and people. Their achievement was more from the common level of human nature than are Emerson's astonishing paradoxes. Yet I believe his work has the seal of immortality upon it as much as that of any of them. No doubt he has a meaning to us now and in this country that will be lost to succeeding time. His religious significance will not be so important to the next generation. He is being or has been so completely absorbed by his times, that readers and hearers hereafter will get him from a thousand sources, or his contribution will become the common property of the race. All the masters probably had some peculiar import or tie to their contemporaries that we at a distance miss. It is thought by scholars that we have lost the key, or one key, to Dante, and Chaucer, and Shakespeare—the key or the insight that people living under the same roof get of each other.

But aside from and over and above everything else, Emerson ***appeals to youth and to genius***. If you have these, you will understand him and delight in him; if not, or neither of them, you will make little of him. And I do not see why this should not be just as true any time hence as at present.

THE FLIGHT OF THE EAGLE.

TO WALT WHITMAN.

" *I, thirty-six years old, in perfect health, begin,*
Hoping to cease not till death."

CHANTS DEMOCRATIC.
" *They say that thou art sick, art growing old,*
Thou Poet of unconquerable health,
With youth fur-stretching, through the golden wealth Of autumn, to Death's
frostful, friendly cold, The never-blenching eyes, that did behold
Life's fair and foul, with measureless content,
And gaze ne'er sated, saddened as they bent Over the dying soldier in the
fold
Of thy large comrade love ;—then broke the tear ! War-dream, field-vigil, the
bequeathed kiss,
Have brought old age to thee; yet. Master, now, Cease not thy song to us; lest
we should miss
A death-chant of indomitable cheer, Blown as a gale from God;—oh, sing it
thou ! "
ARRAN LEIGH (England).

THE FLIGHT OF THE EAGLE.
I

WHOEVER has witnessed the flight of any of the great birds, as the eagle, the
condor, the sea-gulls, the proud hawks, etc., has perhaps felt that the poetic suggestion of the feathered tribes is not all con-lined to the sweet and tiny songsters—the

thrushes, canaries, and mocking-birds of the groves and orchards, or of the gilded cage in my lady's chamber. It is by some such analogy that I would indicate the character of the poetry I am about to discuss—compared with that of the more popular and melodious singer; the poetry of the strong wing and the daring flight.

Well and profoundly has a Danish critic said, in *For I de og Virkelighed* ("For the Idea and the Reality "), a Copenhagen magazine :—

"It may be candidly admitted that the American poet has not the elegance, special melody, nor recherché *aroma of the accepted poets of Europe or his own country; but his compass and general harmony are infinitely greater. The sweetness and spice, the poetic* ennui, the tender longings, the exquisite art-finish of those choice poets are mainly unseen and unmet in him—perhaps because he cannot achieve them—more likely because he disdains them. But there is an electric *living* soul in his poetry, far more fermenting and bracing. His wings do not glitter in their movement from rich and vari-coloured plumage, nor are his notes those of the accustomed song-birds; but his flight is the flight of the eagle."

Yes, there is not only the delighting of the ear with the outpouring of sweetest melody, and its lessons—but there is the delighting of the eye and soul through that soaring and circling in the vast empyrean of "a strong bird on pinions free"—lessons of freedom, power, grace, and spiritual suggestion—vast, unparalleled, formless lessons.

It is now upwards of twenty years since Walt Whitman printed (in 1855) his first thin beginning volume of *Leaves of Grass*; and holding him to the test which he himself early proclaimed, namely, "that the proof of the poet shall be sternly deferred till his country has absorbed him as affectionately as he has absorbed it," he is yet on trial, yet makes his appeal to an indifferent or to a scornful audience. That his complete absorption, however, by his own country, and by the world, is ultimately to take place, is one of the beliefs that grows stronger and stronger within me as time passes, and I suppose it is with a hope to help forward this absorption that I write of him now. Only here and there has he yet effected a lodgment, usually in the younger and more virile minds. But considering the unparalleled audacity of his undertaking, and the absence in most critics and readers of anything like full-grown and robust aesthetic perception, the wonder really is not that he should have made such slow progress, but that he should have gained any foothold at all. The whole literary ***technique*** of the race for the last two hundred years has been squarely against him, laying as it does the emphasis upon form and scholarly endowments instead of upon aboriginal power and manhood.

My own mastery of the poet, incomplete as it is, has doubtless been much facilitated by contact—talks, meals, jaunts, etc. with him, stretching through a decade of years, and by seeing how everything in his ***personnel*** was resumed and carried forward in his literary expression; in fact, how the one was a living commentary upon the other. After the test of time nothing goes home like the test of actual intimacy, and to tell me that Whitman is not a large, fine, fresh, magnetic personality, making you love him, and want always to be with him, were to tell me that my whole past life is a deception, and all the impression of my percep-tives a fraud. I have studied him as I have studied the birds, and have found that the nearer I got to him the more I saw. Nothing about a first-class man can be overlooked; he is to be studied in every feature,—in his physiology and phrenology, in the shape of his head, in his brow, his eye, his glance, his nose, his ear (the ear is as indicative in a man as in a horse), his voice. In Whitman all these things are remarkably striking and suggestive. His face exhibits & rare combination of harmony and sweetness with strength,—strength like the vaults and piers of the Roman architecture. Sculptor never carved a finer ear or a more imaginative brow. Then his heavy-lidded, absorbing eye, his sympathetic voice, and the impression which he makes of starting from the broad bases of the universal human traits. (If Whitman was grand in his physical and perfect health, I think him far more so now (1877) cheerfully mastering paralysis, penury, and old age.) You know on seeing the man and becoming familiar with his presence, that if he achieve the height at all it will be from where every man stands, and not from some special genius, or exceptional and adventitious point. He does not make the impression of the scholar or artist or litterateur, but such as you would imagine the antique heroes to make, that of a sweet-blooded, receptive, perfectly normal, catholic man, with, further than that, a look about him that is best suggested by the word elemental or cosmical. It was this, doubtless, that led Thoreau to write, after an hour's interview, "that he suggested something a little more than human." In fact, the main clew to Walt Whitman's life and personality, and the expression of them in his poems, is to be found in about the largest emotional element that has appeared anywhere. This, if not controlled by a potent rational balance, would either have tossed him helplessly for ever, or wrecked him as disastrously as ever storm and gale drove ship to ruin. These volcanic emotional fires appear everywhere in his books, and it is really these, aroused to intense activity and unnatural strain during the four years of the war, and persistent labours in the hospitals, that have resulted in his illness and paralysis since.

It has been impossible, I say, to resist these personal impressions and magnetisms, and impossible with me not to follow them up in the poems, in doing which I found that his Leaves of Grass was really *the drama of himself* played upon various and successive stages of nature, history, passion, experience, patriotism, etc., and that he had not made, nor had he intended to make, mere excellent "poems," tunes, statues, or statuettes, in the ordinary sense.

Before the man's complete acceptance and assimilation by America, he may have to be first passed down through the minds of critics and commentators, and given to the people with some of his rank new quality taken off—a quality like that which adheres to objects in the open air, and makes them either forbidding or attractive, as one's mood is healthful and robust or feeble and languid. The processes are silently at work. Already seen from a distance, and from other atmospheres and surroundings, he assumes magnitude and orbic coherence; for in curious contrast to the general denial of Whitman in this country (though he has more lovers and admirers here than is generally believed) stands the reception accorded him in Europe. The poets there, almost without exception, recognise his transcendent quality, the men of science his thorough scientific basis, the republicans his inborn democracy, and all his towering picturesque personality and modernness. Prof. Clifford says he is more thoroughly in harmony with the spirit and letter of advanced scientism than any other living poet. Prof. Tyrrell and Mr. Symonds find him eminently Greek, in the sense in which to be natural and " self-regulated by the law of perfect health" is to be Greek. The French ***Revue des Deux Mondes*** pronounces his war poems the most vivid, the most humanly passionate, and the most modern, of all the verse of the nineteenth century. Freiligrath translated him into German, and hailed him as the founder of a new democratic and modern order of poetry, greater than the old. But I do not propose to go over the whole list here; I only wish to indicate that the absorption is well commenced abroad, and that probably her poet will at last reach America, by way of those far-off, roundabout channels. The old mother will first masticate and moisten the food which is still too tough for her offspring.

When I first fell in with Leaves of Grass I was taken by isolated passages scattered here and there through the poems ; these I seized upon, and gave myself no concern about the rest. Single lines in it often went to the bottom of the questions that were vexing me. The following, though less here than when encountered in the frame of mind which the poet begets in you, curiously settled and stratified a certain range of turbid fluctuating inquiry :—

" There was never any more inception than there is now,—
Nor any more youth or age than there is now ;
And will never be any more perfection than there is now,
Nor any more heaven or hell than there is now."
These lines, also, early had an attraction for me I could not define, and were of great service :—

" Pleasantly and well suited I walk,
Whither I walk I cannot define, but I know it is good,
The whole universe indicates that it is good,
The past and the present indicate that it is good."

In the following episode, too, there was to me something far deeper than the words or story:—

"The runaway slave came to my house and stopt outside;
I heard his motions crackling the twigs of the wood-pile;

Through the swung half-door of the kitchen T saw him limpsy and weak,
And went where he sat on a log, and led him in, and assured him,
And brought water and filled a tub for his sweated body and bruised feet,
And gave him a room that entered from my own, and gave him some coarse clean clothes;
And remember perfectly well his revolving eyes and bis awkwardness,
And remember putting plasters on the galls of his neck and ankles :
He stayed with me a week before he was recuperated and passed North;
(I had him sit next me at table—my firelock leaned in the corner)/'

But of the book as a whole I could form no adequate conception, and it was not till many years, and after I had known the poet himself, as already stated, that I saw in it a teeming, rushing globe well worthy my best days and strength to surround and comprehend.

One thing that early took me in the poems was (as before alluded to) the tremendous personal force back of them, and felt through them as the sun through vapour; not merely intellectual grasp or push, but a warm, breathing, towering, magnetic Presence that there was no escape from.

Another fact I was quick to perceive, namely, that this man had almost in excess a quality in which every current poet was lacking I mean the faculty of being in entire sympathy with actual Nature, and the objects and shows of Nature, and of rude, abysmal man; and appalling directness of utterance therefrom, at first-hand, without any intermediate agency or modification.

The influence of books and works of art upon an author may be seen in all respectable writers. If knowledge alone made literature, or culture genius, there would be no dearth of these things among the moderns. But I feel bound to say that there is something higher and deeper than the influence or perusal of any or all books, or all other productions of genius—a quality of information which the masters can never impart, and which all the libraries do not hold. This is the absorption by an author, previous to becoming so, of the spirit of Nature, through the visible objects of the universe, and his affiliation with them subjectively and objectively. Not more surely is the blood quickened and purified by contact with the unbreathed air, than is the spirit of man vitalised and made strong by intercourse with the real things of the earth. The calm, all-permitting, wordless spirit of Nature—yet so eloquent to him who hath ears to hear! The sunrise, the heaving sea, the woods and mountains, the storm and the whistling winds, the gentle summer day, the winter sights and sounds, the night, and the high dome of stars—to have really perused these, especially from childhood onward, till what there is in them, so impossible to define, finds its full mate and echo in the mind—this only is the lore which breathes the breath of life into all the rest. Without it, literary productions may have the superb beauty of statues, but with it only can they have the beauty of life.

I was never troubled at all by what the critics called Whitman's want of art, or his violation of art. I saw that he at once designedly swept away all which the said critics have commonly meant by that term. The dominant impression was of the living presence and voice. He would have no curtains, he said, not the finest, between himself and his reader; and in thus bringing me face to face with his subject I perceived he not only did not escape conventional art, but I perceived an enlarged, enfranchised art in this very abnegation of art. ' When half-gods go, whole gods arrive." It was obvious to me that the new style gained more than it lost, and that in this fullest operatic launching forth of the voice, though it sounded strangely at first, and required the ear to get used to it, there might be quite as much science, and a good deal more power, than in the tuneful but constricted measures we were accustomed to.

To the eye the page of the new poet presented about the same contrast with the page of the popular poets that trees and the free unbidden growths of nature do with a carefully clipped hedge; and to the spirit the contrast was about the same. The hedge is the more studiedly and obviously beautiful, but ah ! there is a kind of beauty and satisfaction in trees that one would not card to lose. There is symmetry and proportion in the sonnet, but to me there is something I would not exchange for them in the wild swing and balance of many unmeasured and unrhymed passages in Shakespeare : like the one for instance in which these lines occur:—

" To be imprisoned in the viewless winds,
And blown with restless violence round
About the pendent world."

Here is the spontaneous grace and symmetry of a forest tree, or a soughing mass of foliage.

And this passage from my poet I do not think could be improved by the verse-maker's art:—

" This day before dawn I ascended a hill and looked at the crowded heaven,
And I said to my Spirit, When we become the enfolders of those orbs, and the pleasure and knowledge of everything in them, shall we be filed and satisfied then
And my Spirit said, No, we but level that lift, to pass and continue beyond."

Such breaking with the routine poetic, and with the grammar of verse, was of coarse a dangerous experiment, and threw the composer absolutely upon his intrinsic merits, upon his innately poetic and rhythmic quality. He must stand or fall by these alone, since he discarded all artificial, all adventitious helps. If interior, spontaneous rhythm could not be relied upon, and the natural music and flexibility of language, then there was nothing to shield the ear from the pitiless hail of words—not one softly padded verse anywhere.

All poets, except those of the very first order, owe immensely to the form, the art, to the stereotyped metres and stock figures they find ready to their hand. The form is suggestive—it invites and aids expression, and lends itself readily, like fashion, to conceal, or extenuate, or eke out poverty of thought and feeling in the verse. The poet can "cut and cover," as the farmer says, in a way the prose-writer never can, nor one whose form is essentially prose, like Whitman's.

I, too, love to see the forms worthily used as they always are by the master; and I have no expectation that they are going out of fashion right away. A great deal of poetry that serves, and helps sweeten one's cup, would be impossible without them— would be nothing when separated from them. It is for the ear and the sense of tune, and of carefully carved and modelled forms, and is not meant to arouse the soul with the taste of power, and to start off on journeys for itself. But the great inspired utterances, like the Bible—what would they gain by being cast in the moulds of metrical verse ?

In all that concerns art, viewed from any high standpoint,—proportion, continence, self-control, unfaltering adherence to natural standards, subordination. of parts, perfect adjustment of the means to the end, obedi-ence to inward law, no trifling, no levity, no straining after effect, impartially attending to the back and loins as well as to the head, and even holding toward his subject an attitude of perfect acceptance and equality,—principles of art to which alone the great spirits are amenable,—in all these respects, I say, this poet is as true as an orb in astronomy.

To his literary expression pitched on scales of such unprecedented breadth and loftiness, the contrast of his personal life comes in with a foil of curious homeliness and simplicity. Perhaps never before has the absolute and average *commonness of humanity* been so steadily and unaffectedly-adhered to. I give here a glimpse of him in Washington on a Navy Yard horse-car, toward the close of the war, one summer day at sundown. The car is crowded and suffocatingly hot, with many passengers on the rear platform, and among them a bearded, florid-faced man, elderly, but agile, resting against the dash, by the side of the young conductor, and evidently his intimate friend. The man wears a broad-brim white hat. Among the jam inside near the door, a young Englishwoman, of the working class, with two children, has had trouble all the way with the youngest, a strong, fat, fretful bright babe of fourteen or fifteen months, who bids fair to worry the mother completely out, besides becoming a howling nuisance to everybody. As the car tugs around Capitol Hill the young one is more demoniac than ever, and the flushed and perspiring mother is just ready to burst into tears with weariness and vexation. The car stops at the top of the hill to let off most of the rear platform passengers, and the white-hatted man reaches inside and gently but firmly disengaging the babe from its stifling place in the mother's arms, takes it in his own, and out in the air. The astonished and excited child, partly in fear, partly in satisfaction at the change, stops its screaming, and as the man adjusts it more securely to his breast, plants its chubby hands against him, and pushing off as far as it can, gives a good long look squarely in his face —then, as if satisfied, snuggles down with its head on his neck, and in less than a minute is sound and peacefully asleep without another whimper, utterly fagged out. A square or so more and the conductor, who has had an unusually hard and uninterrupted day's work, gets off for his first meal and relief since morning. And now the white-hatted man, holding the slumbering babe also, acts as conductor the rest of the distance, keeping his eye on the passengers inside, who have by this time thinned out greatly. He makes a very good conductor, too, pulling the bell to stop or go on as needed, and seems to enjoy the occupation. The babe meanwhile rests its fat cheeks close on his neck and grey beard, one of his arms vigilantly surrounding it, while the other signals, from time to time, with the strap; and the flushed mother inside has a good half-hour to breathe, and cool, and recover herself.

No poem of our day dates and locates itself as absolutely as " Leave, of Grass;" but suppose it had been written three or four centuries ago, and had located itself in mediaeval Europe, and was now first brought to light, together with a history of Walt Whitman's simple and disinterested life, can there be any doubt about the cackling that would at once break out in the whole brood of critics over the golden egg that had been uncovered ? This I reckon would be a favourite passage with all:—

" Yon sea ! I resign myself to you also—I guess what you mean;
I behold from the beach your crooked inviting fingers;
I believe you refuse to go back without feeling of me ;
We must have a turn together—I undress-hurry me out of sight of the land;
Cushion me soft, rock me in billowy drowse;
Dash me with amorous wet—I can repay you.

" Sea of stretched ground-swells !
Sea breathing broad and convulsive breaths !
Sea of the brine of life ! sea of unshovelled yet always ready graves !

Howler and scooper of storms! eapricious and dainty sea!
I am integral with you—I too am of one phase, and of all phases."

This other passage would afford many a text for the moralists and essayists :—

"Of persons arrived at high positions, ceremonies, wealth, scholarship, and the like;
To me, all that those persons have arrived at sinks away from them, except as it results to their Bodies and Souls,
So that often to me they appear gaunt and naked,
And often to me, each one mocks the others, and mocks himself or herself,
And of each one, the core of life, namely happiness, is full of the rotten excrement of maggots;
And often, to me, those men and women pass unwittingly the true realities of life, and go toward false realities,
And often to me they are alive after what custom has served them, but nothing more,
And often to me, they are sad, hasty, unwaked somnambules, walking the dusk."
Ah, Time, you enchantress! what tricks you play with us ! The old is already proved —the past and the distant hold nothing but the beautiful.

It is not so much of fatty degeneration that we are in danger in America, as of calcareous. The fluids, moral and physical, are evaporating, surfaces are becoming encrusted, there is a deposit of flint in the veins and arteries, outlines are abnormally sharp and hard, nothing is held in solution, all is precipitated in well-defined ideas and opinions.

But when I think of the type of character planted and developed by my poet, I think of a man or woman rich above all things in the genial human attributes, one "nine times folded " in an atmosphere of tenderest, most considerate humanity, an atmosphere warm with the breath of a tropic heart, that makes your buds of affection and of genius start and unfold like a south wind in May. Your intercourse with such a character is not merely intellectual; it is deeper and better than that. Walter Scott carried such a fund of sympathy and good-will that even the animals found fellowship with him, and the pigs understood his great heart

It was the large endowment of Whitman, in his own character, in this respect, that made his services in the army hospitals, during the war, so ministering and effective, and that renders his "Drum-taps " the tenderest and most deeply yearning and sorrowful expression of the human heart in poetry that ever war called forth. Indeed, from my own point of view, there is no false or dangerous tendency among us, in life or in letters, that this poet does not offset and correct. Fret and chafe as much as we will, we are bound to gravitate, more or less, toward this mountain, and feel its bracing, rugged air.

Without a certain self-surrender there is no greatness possible in literature, any more than in religion, or in anything else. It is always a trait of the master, that he is not afraid of being compromised by the company he keeps. He is the central and main fact in any company. Nothing so lowly but he will do it reverence ; nothing so high but he can stand in its presence. His theme is the river, and he the ample and willing channel. Little natures love to disparage and take down; they do it in self-defence, but the master gives you all, and more than your due. Whitman does not stand aloof, superior, a priest or a critic; he abandons himself to all the strong human currents; he enters into and affiliates with every phase of life; he bestows himself royally upon whoever and whatever will receive him. There is no competition between himself and his subject; he is not afraid of overpraising, or making too much of the commonest individual. What exalts others exalts him.

We have had great help in Emerson in certain ways—first-class service. He probes the conscience and the moral purpose as few men have done, and gives much needed stimulus there. But after him, the need is all the more pressing for a broad, powerful, opulent, human personality to absorb these ideals, and make something more of them than fine sayings. With Emerson alone we are rich in sunlight, but poor in rain and dew—poor, too, in soil, and in the moist, gestating earth principle.

Emerson's tendency is not to broaden and enrich, but to concentrate and refine.

Then, is there not an excessive modesty, without warrant in philosophy or nature, dwindling us in this country, drying us up in the viscera? Is there not a decay—a deliberate, strange abnegation and dread— of sane sexuality, of maternity and paternity, among us, and in our literary ideals and social types of men and women ? For myself I welcome any evidence to the contrary, or any evidence that deeper and counteracting agencies are at work, as unspeakably precious. I do not know where this evidence is furnished in such ample measure as in the pages of Walt Whitman. The great lesson of Nature, I take it, is that a sane sensuality must be preserved at all hazards, and this, it seems to me, is also the great lesson of his writings. The point is fully settled in him, that however they may have been held in abeyance, or restricted to other channels, there is still sap and fecundity, and depth of virgin soil in the race, sufficient to produce a man of the largest mould, and the most audacious and unconquerable egoism, and on a plane the last to be reached by these qualities ; a man of antique stature, of Greek fibre and gripe, with science and the modern added, without abating one jot or tittle of his native force, adhesiveness, Americanism, and democracy.

As I have already hinted, Whitman has met with by far his amplest acceptance and appreciation in Europe. There is good reason for this, though it is not what has been generally claimed, namely, that the cultivated classes of Europe are surfeited with respectability, half dead with ennui and routine, etc., and find an agreeable change in the daring unconventionality of the new poet. For the fact is, it is not the old and jaded minds of London, or Paris, or Dublin, or Copenhagen, that have acknowledged him, but the fresh, eager, young minds. Nine-tenths of his admirers there are the sturdiest men in the fields of art, science, and literature.

In many respects, as a race, we Americans have been pampered and spoiled; we have been brought up on sweets. I suppose that, speaking literally, no people under the sun consume so much confectionery, so much pastry and cake, or indulge in so many gassy and sugared drinks. The soda-fountain, with its syrups, has got into literature, and furnishes the popular standard of poetry. The old heroic stamina of our ancestors, that craved the bitter but nourishing homebrewed, has died out, and in its place there is a sickly cadaverousness that must be pampered and corseted. Among educated people here there is a mania for the bleached, the double refined; white houses, white china, white marble, and white skins. We take the bone and sinew out of the flour in order to have white bread, and are bolting our literature as fast as possible.

It is for these and kindred reasons that Walt Whitman is more read abroad than in his own country. It is on the rank, human, and emotional side—sex, magnetism, health, physique, etc.that he is so full. Then his receptivity and assimilative powers are enormous, and he demands these in his reader. In fact, his poems are physiological as much as they are intellectual. They radiate from his entire being, and are charged to repletion with that blended quality of mind and body —psychic and physiologic—which the living form and presence send forth. Never before in poetry has the body received such ennoblement. The great theme is IDENTITY, and identity comes through the body; and all that pertains to the body, the poet teaches, is entailed upon the spirit. In his rapt gaze the body and the soul are one, and what debases the one debases the other. Hence he glorifies the body. Not more ardently and purely did the great sculptors of antiquity carve it in the enduring marble, than this poet has celebrated it in his masculine and flowing lines. The bearing of his work in this direction is invaluable. Well has it been said that the man or woman who has Leaves of Grass for a daily companion will be under the constant, invisible influence of sanity, cleanliness, strength, and a gradual severance from all that corrupts and makes morbid and mean.

In regard to the unity and construction of the poems, the reader sooner or later discovers the true solution to be, that the dependence, cohesion, and final reconciliation of the whole are in the Personality of the poet himself. As in Shakespeare everything is strung upon the plot, the play, and loses when separated from it, so in this poet every line and sentence refers to and necessitates the Personality behind it, and derives its chief significance therefrom. In other words, " Leaves of Grass " is essentially a dramatic poem, a free representation of man in his relation to the outward world,—the play, the interchanges between him and it, apart from social and artificial considerations—in which we discern the central purpose or thought to be for every man and woman his or her Individuality, and around that Nationality. To show rather than to tell,—to body forth as in a play how these arise and blend, how the man is developed and recruited, his spirit's descent; how he walks through materials absorbing and conquering them ; how he confronts the immensities of time and space ; where are the true sources of his power, the soul's real riches—that which "adheres and goes forward, and is not dropped by death;" how he is all defined and published and made certain through his body; the value of health and physique; the great solvent, Sympathy,—to show the need of larger and fresher types in art and in life, and then how the State is compacted, and how the democratic idea is ample and composite, and cannot fail us,—to show all this, I say, not as in a lecture or critique, but suggestively and inferentially,—to work it out freely and picturesquely, with endless variations, with person and picture and parable and adventure, is the lesson and object of " Leaves of Grass." From the first line, where the poet says,

" I loafe and invite my Soul,"

to the last, all is movement and fusion—all is clothed in flesh and blood. The scene changes, the curtain rises and falls, but the theme is still Man,—his opportunities, his relations, his past, his future, his sex, his pride in himself, his omnivorousness, his "great hands," his yearning heart, his seething brain, the abysmal depths that underlie him and open from him, etc., all illustrated in the poet's own character. Himself is the chief actor always. His personality directly facing you, and with its eye steadily upon you, runs through every page, spans all the details, and rounds and completes them, and compactly holds them. This gives the form and the art conception, and gives homogeneousness.

When Tennyson sends out a poem, it is perfect, like an apple or a peach; slowly wrought out and dismissed, it drops from his boughs holding a conception or an idea that spheres it and makes it whole. It is completed, distinct, and separate,—might be his, or might be any man's. It carries his quality, but it is a thing of itself, and centres and depends upon itself. Whether or not the world will hereafter consent, as in the past, to call only beautiful creations of this sort poems, remains to be seen. But this is certainly not what Walt Whitman does, or aims to do, except in a few cases. He completes no poems, apart and separate from himself, and his pages abound in hints to that effect :—

"Let others finish specimens—I never finish specimens;
I shower them by exhaustless laws, as Nature does, fresh and modern continually."

His lines are pulsations, thrills, waves of force, indefinite dynamics, formless, constantly emanating from the living centre, and they carry the quality of the author's personal presence with them in a way that is unprecedented in literature.

Occasionally there is a poem or a short piece that detaches itself and assumes something like ejaculatory and statuesque proportion, as "O Captain, my Captain," "Pioneers," "Beat, Beat, Drums," and others in " Drum-Taps ;" but all the great poems, like " Walt Whitman," " Song of the Open Road," "Crossing Brooklyn Ferry," "To Working Men," "Sleep-chasings," etc., are out-flamings, out-rushings of the pent fires of the poet's soul. The first-named poem, which is the seething, dazzling sun of his subsequent poetic system, shoots in rapid succession waves of almost consuming energy. It is indeed a central orb of fiercest light and heat, swept by wild storms of emotion, but at the same time of sane and beneficent potentiality. Neither in it nor in either of the others is there the building up of a fair verbal structure, a symmetrical piece of mechanism, whose last stone is implied and necessitated in the first.

"The critic's great error," says Heine, "lies in asking 'What ought the artist to do?' It would be far more correct to ask, 4 What does the artist intend ?'" It is probably partly because his field is so large, his demands so exacting, his method so new (necessarily so), and from the whole standard of the poems being what I may call an astronomical one, that the critics complain so generally of want of form in him. And the critics are right enough, as far as their objection goes. There is no deliberate form here, any more than there is in the forces of nature. Shall we say, then, that nothing but the void exists? The void is filled by a Presence. There is a controlling, directing, overarching will in every page, every verse, that there is no escape from. Design and purpose, natural selection, growth, culmination, etc., are just as pronounced as in any poet.

There is a want of form in the unfinished statue, because it is struggling into form ; it is nothing without form; but there is no want of form in the elemental laws and effusions—in fire or water, or rain, or dew, or the smell of the shore, or the plunging waves. And may there not be the analogue of this in literature—a potent, quickening, exhilarating quality in words, apart from and without any consideration of constructive form ? Under the influence of the expansive, creative force that plays upon me from these pages, like sunlight or gravitation, the question of form never comes up, because I do not for one moment escape the eye, the source from which the power and action emanate.

I know that Walt Whitman has written many passages with reference far more to their position, interpretation, and scanning ages hence, than for current reading. Much of his material is too near us ; it needs time. Seen through the vista of long years, perhaps centuries, it will assume quite different hues. Perhaps those long lists of trades; tools, and occupations, would not be so repellent if we could read them as we read Homer's catalogue of the ships, through the retrospect of ages. They are justified in the poem aside from their historic value, because they are alive and full of action,—panoramas of the whole mechanical and industrial life of America, north, east, south, west,—bits of scenery, bird's-eye views, glimpses of moving figures, caught as by a flash, char-: acteristic touches in-doors and out, all passing in quick succession before you. They have in the fullest measure what Lessing demands in poetry, the quality of ebbing and flowing action, as distinct from the dead water of description—they are thoroughly dramatic, fused, pliant, and obedient to the poet's will No glamour is thrown over them, no wash of sentiment; and if they have not the charm of novelty and distance, why that is an accident that bars them in a measure to us, but not to the future.

Very frequently in these lists or enumerations of objects, actions, shows, etc., there are sure to occur lines of perfect description :—

"Where the heifers browse—where geese nip their food with short jerks;
Where sundown shadows lengthen over the limitless and lonesome prairie;
Where herds of buffalo make a crawling spread of the square miles far and near;
Where the splash of swimmers and divers cools the warm noon ;
Where the katydid works her chromatic reed on the walnut-tree over the well."

"Spar-makers in the spar-yard, the swarming row of well-grown apprentices,
The swing of their axes on the square-hewed log, shaping it toward the shape of a mast,
The brisk short crackle of the steel driven slantingly into the pine,
The butter-coloured chips flying off in great flakes and slivers,
The limber motion of the brawny young arms and hips in easy costumes."

" Always these compact lands—lands tied at the hips with the belt stringing the huge oval lakes."

" Far breath'd land ! Arctic braced! Mexican breezed I—the diverse ! the compact!"

Tried by the standards of the perfect statuesque poems, these pages will indeed seem strange enough ; but viewed as a part of the poetic compend of America, the swift gathering in from her wide-spreading, multitudinous, material life, of traits and points and suggestions that belong here and are characteristic, they have their value. The poet casts his great seine into events and doings and material progress, and these are some of the fish, not all beautiful by any means, but all terribly alive, and all native to these waters.

In the " Carol of Occupations " occur, too, those formidable inventories of the more heavy and coarse-grained trades and tools that few if any readers have been able to stand before, and that have given the scoffers and caricaturists their favourite weapons. If you detach a page of these, and ask, "Is it poetry? have the 'hoghook,' the 'killing hammer,' the 'cutter's cleaver,' ' the packer's maul,' etc., met with a change of heart, and been converted into celestial cutlery ? " I answer, No, they are as barren of poetry as a desert of grass; but in their place in the poem, and in the collection, they serve as masses of shade or neutral colour in pictures, or in nature, or character—a negative service, but still indispensable. The point, the moral of the poem, is really backed up and driven home by this list. The poet is determined there shall be no mistake about it. He will not put in the dainty and pretty things merely, he will put in the coarse and common things also, and he swells the list till even his robust muse begins to look uneasy. Remember, too, that Whitman declaredly writes the lyrics of America, of the masses, of democracy, and of the practical labour of mechanics, boatmen, and farmers :—

"The sum of all known reverence I add up in you, whoever you are;

All doctrines, all politics and civilisation, exude from you;

All sculpture and monuments, and anything inscribed anywhere are tallied in you;

The gist of histories and statistics as far back as the records reach, is in you this hour,

and myths and tales the same:

If you were not breathing and walking here, where would they all be ?

The most renown'd poems would be ashes,

orations and plays would be vacuums.

All architecture is what you do to it when you look upon it;

(Did you think it was in the white or grey stone ? or the lines of the arches and cornices ?)

All music is what awakens from you when you are reminded by the instruments ;

It is not the violins and the cornets—it is not the oboe, nor the beating drums—nor the score of the baritone singer singing his sweet romanza nor that of the men's chorus, nor that of the women's chorus,

It is nearer and further than they."

Out of this same spirit of reverence for man and all that pertains essentially to him, and the steady ignoring of conventional and social distinctions and prohibitions, and on the same plane as the universal brotherhood of the poems, come those passages in "Leaves of Grass " that have caused so much abuse and fury,—the allusions to sexual acts andorgans,—the momentary contemplation of man as the perpetuator of his species. Many good judges who have followed Whitman thus far, stop here and refuse their concurrence. But if the poet has failed in this part he has failed in the rest. It is of a piece with the whole. He has felt in his way the same necessity as that which makes the anatomist or physiologist not pass by, or neglect, or falsify, the loins of his typical personage. All the passages and allusions that come under this head have a scientific coldness and purity, but differ from science, as poetry always must differ, in being alive and sympathetic, instead of dead and analytic. There is nothing of the forbidden here, none of those sweet morsels that we love to roll under the tongue, such as are found in Byron and Shakespeare, and even in austere Dante. If the fact is not lifted up and redeemed by the solemn and far-reaching laws of maternity and paternity, through which the poet alone contemplates it, then it is irredeemable, and one side of our nature is intrinsically vulgar and mean.

Again: Out of all the full-grown, first-class poems, no matter what their plot or theme, emerges a sample of Man, each after its kind, its period, its nationality, its antecedents. The vast and cumbrous Hindu epics contribute their special types of both man and woman, impossible except from far-off Asia and Asian antiquity. Out of Homer, after all his gorgeous action and events, the distinct personal identity, the heroic and warlike chieftain of Hellas only permanently remains. In the same way, when the fire and fervour of Shakespeare's plots and passions subside, the special feudal personality, as lord or gentleman, still towers in undying vitality. Even the Sacred Writings themselves, considered as the first great poems, leave on record, out of all the rest, the portraiture of a characteristic Oriental Man. Far different from these (and yet as he says, "the same old countenance pensively looking forth," and "the same red running blood"), "Leaves of Grass" and "Two Rivulets" also bring their contribution,—nay, behind every page *that* is the main purport—to outline a New World Man and a New World Woman, modern, complete, democratic, not only fully and nobly intellectual and spiritual, but in the same measure physical, emotional, and even fully and nobly carnal.

An acute person once said to me, "As I read and re-read these poems. I more and more think their inevitable result in time must be to produce

'*A race of splendid and savage old men,*'

of course dominated by moral and spiritual laws, but with volcanoes of force always alive beneath the surface."

And still again: One of the questions to be put to any poem assuming a first-class importance among us—and I especially invite this inquiry toward " Leaves of Grass "—is, how far is this work consistent with, and the outcome of, that something which secures to the race ascendency, empire, and perpetuity ? There is in every dominant people a germ, a quality, an expansive force that, no matter how it is overlaid, gives them their push and their hold upon existence— writes their history upon the earth, and stamps their imprint upon the age. To what extent is your masterpiece the standard-bearer of this quality—helping the race to victory? helping me to be more myself than I otherwise would ?

III.

Not the least of my poet's successes is in his thorough assimilation of the modern sciences, transmuting them into strong poetic nutriment, and the extent to which all his main poems are grounded in the deepest principles of modern philosophical inquiry.

Nearly all the old literatures may be said to have been founded upon fable, and upon a basis and even superstructure of ignorance, that, however charming it may be, we have not now got, and could not keep if we had. The bump of wonder, the feeling of the marvellous, a kind of half pleasing fear, like that of children in the dark or in the woods, were largely operative with the old poets, and I believe are necessary to any eminent success in this field; but they seem nearly to have died out of the modern mind, like organs there is no longer any use for. The poetic temperament has not yet adjusted itself to the new lights, to science, and to the vast fields and expanses opened up in the physical cosmos by astronomy and geology, and in the spiritual or intellectual world by the great German metaphysicians. The staple of a large share of our poetic literature is yet mainly the result of the long age of fable and myth that now lies behind us. " Leaves of Grass " is, perhaps, the first serious and large attempt at an expression in poetry of a knowledge of the earth as one of the orbs, and of man as a microcosm of the whole, and to give to the imagination these new and true fields of wonder and romance. In it fable and superstition are at an end, priestcraft is at an end, scepticism and doubt are at an end, with all the misgivings and dark forebodings that have dogged the human mind since it began to relax its hold upon tradition and the past—and we behold man reconciled, happy, ecstatic, full of reverence, awe, and wonder, reinstated in Paradise—the paradise of perfect knowledge and unrestricted faith.

It needs but a little pondering to see that the great poet of the future will not be afraid of science, but will rather seek to plant his feet upon it as upon a rock. He knows that from an enlarged point of view there is no feud between Science and Poesy, any more than there is between Science and Religion, or between Science and Life. He sees that the poet and the scientist do not travel opposite, but parallel roads, that often approach each other very closely, if they do not at times actually join. The poet will always pause when he finds himself in opposition to science, and the scientist is never more worthy the name than when he escapes from analysis into synthesis, and gives us living wholes. And science, in its present bold and receptive mood, may be said to be eminently creative, and to have made every first-class thinker and every large worker in any aesthetic or spiritual field immeasurably its debtor. It has dispelled many illusions, but it has more than compensated the imagination by the unbounded vistas it has opened up on either hand. It has added to our knowledge, but it has added to our ignorance in the same measure; the large circle of light only reveals the larger circle of darkness that encompasses it. and life and being and the orbs are enveloped in a greater mystery to the poet to-day than they were in the times of Homer or Isaiah. Science, therefore, does not restrict the imagination, but often compels it to longer flights. The conception of the earth as an orb shooting like a midnight meteor through space, a brand cast by the burning sun with the fire at its heart still unquenched, the sun itself shooting and carrying the whole train of worlds with it, no one knows whither— what a lift has science given the imagination in this field. Or the tremendous discovery of the correlation and conservation of forces,the identity and convertibility of heat and force and motion, and that no ounce of power is lost, but for ever passed along, changing form but not essence, is a poetic discovery no less than a scientific one. The poets have always felt that it must be so, and when the fact was authoritatively announced by science, every profound poetic mind must have felt a thrill of pleasure. Or the nebular hypothesis of the solar system—it seems the conception of some inspired madman, like William Blake, rather than the cool conclusion of reason, and to carry its own justification, as great power always does. Indeed, our interest in astronomy and geology is essentially a poetic one,—the love of the marvellous, of the sublime, and of grand harmonies. The scientific conception of the sun is strikingly Dantesque, and appals the imagination. Or the hell of fire through which the earth has passed, and the aeons of monsters from which its fair forms have emerged,—from which of the seven circles of the *Inferno* did the scientist get his hint? Indeed, science everywhere reveals a carnival of mightier gods than those that cut such fantastic tricks in the ancient world. Listen to Tyndall on light, or Youmans on the chemistry of a sunbeam, and see how fable pales its ineffectual fires, and the boldest dreams of the poets are eclipsed.

The vibratory theory of light and its identity with the laws of sound, the laws of the tides and the seasons, the wonders of the spectroscope, the theory of gravitation, of electricity, of chemical affinity, the deep beneath deep of the telescope, the world within world of the microscope, etc., —in these and many other fields it is hard to tell whether it is the scientist or the poet we are listening to. What greater magic than that you can take a colourless ray of light, break it across a prism, and catch upon a screen all the divine hues of the rainbow ?

In some respects science has but followed out and confirmed the dim foreshad-owings of the human breast. Man in his simplicity has called the sun father and the earth mother. Science shows this to be no fiction, but a reality ; that we are really children of the sun, and that every heart-beat, every pound of force we exert, is a solar emanation. The power with which you now move and breathe came from the sun just as literally as the bank-notes in your pocket came from the bank.

The ancients fabled the earth as resting upon the shoulders of Atlas, and Atlas as standing upon a turtle ; but what the turtle stood upon was a puzzle. An acute personsays that science has but changed the terms of the equation, but that the unknown quantity is the same as ever. The earth now rests upon the sun—in his outstretched palm; the sun rests upon some other sun, and that upon some other; but what they all finally rest upon, who can tell? Well may Tennyson speak of the " fairy tales of science," and well may Walt Whitman say—

"I lie abstracted, and hear beautiful tales of things, and the reasons of things;
They are so beautiful, I nudge myself to listen."

But making all due acknowledgments to science, there is one danger attend-ing it that the poet can alone save us from,—the danger that science, absorbed with its great problems, will forget Man. Hence, the especial office of the poet with reference to science is to endow it with a human interest. The heart has been dis-enchanted by having disclosed to it blind abstract forces where it had enthroned personal humanistic divinities.. In the old time man was the centre of the system; everything was interested in him, and took sides for or against him. There were nothing but men and gods in the universe. But in the results of science the world is more and more, and man is less and less. The poet must come to the rescue, and place man again at the top, magnify him, exalt him, reinforce him, and match these wonders from without with equal wonders from within. Welcome to the bard who is not appalled by the task, and who can readily assimilate and turn into human emotions these vast deductions of the savans ! The minor poets do nothing in this direction; only men of the largest calibre and most heroic fibre are adequate to the service. Hence, one finds in Tennyson a vast deal more science than he would at first suspect; but it is under his feet; it is no longer science, but faith, or reverence, or poetic nutriment. It is in "Locksley Hall," "The Princess," "In Memoriam," "Maud," and in others of his poems. Here is a passage from "In Memoriam :"—

" They say, The sordid earth whereon we tread

In tracts of fluent heat began
And grew to seeming random forms,
The seeming prey of cyclic storms,
Till at the last arose the man,

Who throve and branched from clime to clime,
The herald of a higher race,
And of himself in higher place,
If so he types this work of time

Within himself, from more to more ;
Or, crowned with attributes of woe,
Like glories, move his course, and show
That life is not as idle ore,

But iron dug from central gloom,
And heated hot with burning fears,
And dipt in baths of hissing tears,
And battered with the shocks of doom

To shape and use. Arise and fly
The reeling Faun, the sensual feast;
Move upward, working out the beast,
And let the ape and tiger die."

Or in this stanza behold how the science is disguised or turned into the sweetest music :—

> " Move eastward, happy earth, and leave
> Yon orange sunset waning slow;
> From fringes of the faded eve,
> 0 happy planet, eastward go;
> Till over thy dark shoulder glow
> Thy silver sister-world, and rise
> To glass herself in dewy eyes
> That watch me from the glen below."

A recognition of the planetary system, and of the great fact that the earth moves eastward through the heavens, in a soft and tender love-song!

But in Walt Whitman alone do we find the full, practical absorption and re-departure therefrom, of the astounding idea that the earth is a star in the heavens like the rest, and that man, as the crown and finish, carries in his moral consciousness the flower, the outcome of all this wide field of turbulent unconscious Nature. Of course in his handling it is no longer science, or rather, it is science dissolved in the fervent heat of the poet's heart, and charged with emotion. "The words of true poems," he says, "are the tufts and final applause of science." Before Darwin or Spencer he proclaimed the doctrine of evolution :—

> " I am stuccoed with quadrupeds and birds all over,
> And have distanced what is behind me for good reasons,
> And call anything close again when I desire it
>
> In vain the speeding and shyness,
> In Tain the plutonic rocks send their old heat against my approach;
> In vain the mastodon retreats beneath his own powdered bones;
> In vain objects stand leagues off, and assume manifold shapes;
> In vain the ocean settling in hollows, and the great monsters lying low."

In the following passage the idea is more fully carried out, and man is viewed through a vista which science alone has laid open, yet how absolutely a work of the creative imagination is revealed :—

" I am an acme of things accomplished, and I
am encloser of things to be.
My feet strike an apex of the apices of the stairs ;
On every step bunches of ages, and larger bunches between the steps;
All below duly travelled, and still I mount and mount.

Rise after rise bow the phantoms behind me;
Afar down I see the huge first Nothing—I know I was even there;
I waited unseen and always, and slept through the lethargic mist,
And took my time, and took no hurt from the foetid carbon.

Long I was hugged close—long and long,
Immense have been the preparations for me,
Faithful and friendly the arms that have helped me,
Cycles ferried my cradle, rowing and rowing like cheerful boatmen;
For room to me stars kept aside in their own rings;
They sent influences to look after what was to hold me.
Before I was born out of my mother, generations guided me;
My embryo has never been torpid—nothing could overlay it,
For it the nebula cohered to an orb,
The long slow strata piled to rest it on,
Vast vegetables gave it sustenance,
Monstrous sauroids transported it in their
mouths, and deposited it with care ;
All forces have been steadily employed to complete and delight me:
Now on this spot I stand with my robust Soul."

I recall no single line of poetry in the language that fills my imagination like that beginning the third verse :—

"Rise after rise how the phantoms behind me. "

One seems to see those huge Brocken shadows of the past sinking and dropping below the horizon like mountain peaks, as he presses onward on his journey.

Akin to this absorption of science is another quality in my poet not found in the rest, except perhaps a mere hint of it now and then in Lucretius—a quality easier felt than described. It is a tidal wave of emotion running all through the poems, which is now and then crested with such passages as this :—

" I am he that walks with the tender and growing night; I call to the earth and sea, half held by the night.
Press close, bare-bosomed night! Press close, magnetic, nourishing night!
Night of south winds ! night of the large, few stars !
Still, nodding night 1 mad, naked, summer night!
Smile, O voluptuous, cool-breath'd earth !
Earth of the slumbering and liquid trees ! Earth of departed sunset! Earth of the mountains, misty topped!
Earth of the vitreous pour of the full moon, just tinged -with blue !
Earth of shine and dark, mottling the tide of the river!
Earth of the limpid grey of clouds, brighter and clearer for my sake !
Far-swooping, elbow'd earth ! rich apple blossom'd earth! Smile, for your lover comes !"

Professor Clifford calls it "cosmic emotion "—a poetic thrill and rhapsody in contemplating the earth as a whole—its chemistry and vitality, its bounty, its beauty, its power, and the applicability of its laws and principles to human, aesthetic and art products. It affords the key to the theory of art upon which Whitman's poems are projected, and accounts for what several critics call their sense of magnitude" Something of the vastness of the succession of objects in Nature."

"I swear there is no greatness or power that does not emulate those of the earth!

T swear there can be no theory of any account, unless it corroborate the theory of the earth!

No politics, art, religion, behaviour, or what not, is of account, unless it compare with the amplitude of the earth,
Unless it face the exactness, vitality, impartiality, rectitude of the earth."

Or again in his " Laws for Creation :"—

" All must have reference to the ensemble of the world, and the compact truth of the world ;
There shall be no subject too pronounced—All works shall illustrate the divine law of indirections."

Indeed, the earth ever floats in this poet's mind as his mightiest symbol—his type of completeness and power. It is the armoury from which he draws his most potent weapons. See, especially, "To the Sayers of Words," " This Compost," " The Song of the Open Road," and "Pensive on her Dead gazing I heard the Mother of all."

The poet holds essentially the same attitude towards cosmic humanity, well illustrated in "Salut au Monde.'

" My spirit has pass'd in compassion and determination around the whole earth ;

I have look'd for equals and lovers, and found them ready for me in all lands;
I think some divine rapport has equalised me with them.
O vapours! I think I have risen with you and moved away to distant continents, and fallen down there for reasons;

I think I have blown with you, 0 winds ;
0 waters, I have finger'd every shore with you."

Indeed, the whole book is leavened with vehement Comradeship. Not only in the relations of individuals to each other shall loving good-will exist and be cultivated— not only between the different towns and cities, and all the States of this indissoluble compacted Union—but it shall make a tie of fraternity and fusion holding all the races and peoples and countries of the whole earth.

Then the National question. As Whitman's completed works now stand, in their two volumes, it is certain they could only have grown out of the Secession War; and they will probably go to future ages, as in literature the most characteristic identification of that war risen from and portraying it, representing its sea of passions and progresses, partaking of all its fierce movements and perturbed emotions, and yet sinking the mere military parts of that war, great as those were, below and with matters far greater, deeper, more human, more expanding, and more enduring.

I must not close this paper without some reference to Walt Whitman's prose writings, which are scarcely less important than his poems. Never has Patriotism— never has the antique Love of Country, with even doubled passion and strength, been more fully expressed, than in these contributions. They comprise two thin volumes—now included in ***Two Rivulets***—called ***Democratic Vistas, and Memoranda during the War***; the former exhibiting the personality of the poet in more vehement and sweeping action even than the poems, and affording specimens of soaring vaticination and impassioned appeal, impossible to match in the literature of our time. The only living author suggested is Carlyle, but so much is added, the ***presence*** is so much more vascular and human, and the whole page so saturated with faith and love and democracy, that even the great Scotchman is overborne. Whitman, too, radiates belief, while at the core of Carlyle's utterances is despair. The style here is eruptive and complex, or what Jeremy Taylor calls ***ayglomerative***, and puts the Addisonian models utterly to rout,—a style such as only the largest and most Titanic workman could effectively use. A sensitive lady of my acquaintance says reading the ***Vistas*** is like being expoaed to a pouring hail-storm,—the words fairly bruise her mind. In its literary construction the book is indeed a shower, or a succession of showers, multitudinous, wide-stretching, down-pouring—the wrathful bolt and the quick veins of poetic fire lighting up the page from time to time. I can easily conceive how certain minds must be swayed and bent by some of these long involved but firm and vehement passages. I cannot deny myself the pleasure of quoting one or two pages. The writer is referring to the great literary relics of past times :—

"For us, along the great highways of time, those monuments stand—those forms of majesty and beauty. For us those beacons burn through all the nights. Unknown Egyptians, graving hieroglyphs ; Hindus, with hymn and apothegm and endless epic; Hebrew prophet, with spirituality, as in flames of lightning, conscience like red-hot iron, plaintive songs and screams of vengeance for tyrannies and enslavement; Christ, with bent head, brooding love and peace, like a dove; Greek, creating eternal shapes of physical and aesthetic proportion ; Roman, lord of satire, the sword, and the codex,—of the figures, some far off and veiled, others near and visible; Dante, stalking with lean form, nothing but fibre, not a grain of superfluous flesh; Angelo, and the great painters, architects, musicians; rich Shakespeare, luxuriant as the sun, artist and singer of Feudalism in its sunset, with all the gorgeous colours, owner thereof, and using them at will; and so to such as German Kant and Hegel, where they, though near us, leaping over the ages, sit again, impassive, imperturbable, like the Egyptian gods. Of these, and the like of these, is it too much, indeed, to return to our favourite figure, and view them as orbs, moving in free paths in the spaces of that other heaven, the cosmic intellect, the Soul ?

" Ye powerful and resplendent ones ! ye were, in your atmospheres, grown not for America, but rather for her foes, the Feudal and the old-while our genius is democratic and modern. Yet could ye, indeed, but breathe your breath of life into our New World's nostrils—not to enslave us as now, but, for our needs, to breed a spirit like your own perhaps (dare we to say it ?) to dominate, even destroy what you yourselves have left! On your plane, and no less, but even higher and wider, will I mete and measure for our wants to-day, and here. I demand races of orbic bards, with unconditional, uncompromising sway. Come forth, sweet democratic despots of the west!"

Here is another passage of a political cast, but showing the same great pinions and lofty flight:—

"It seems as if the Almighty had spread before this nation charts of imperial destinies, dazzling as the sun, yet with lines of blood, and many a deep intestine difficulty, and human aggregate of cankerous imperfection,—Saying, Lo! the roads, the only plans of development, long, and varied with all terrible balks and ebullitions. You said in your soul, I will be empire of empires, overshadowing all else, past and present, putting the history of Old World dynasties, conquests, behind me as of no account —making a new history, the history of Democracy, making old history a dwarf—I alone inaugurating largeness, culminating time. If these, 0 lands of America, are indeed the prizes, the determinations of your Soul, be it so. But behold the cost, and already specimens of the cost Behold, the anguish of suspense, existence itself wavering in the balance, uncertain whether to rise or fall; already close behind you and around you, thick winrows of corpses on battlefields, countless maimed and sick in hospitals, treachery among Generals, folly in the Executive and Legislative departments, schemers, thieves everywhere—cant, credulity, make-believe everywhere. Thought you greatness was to ripen for you, like a pear? If you would have greatness, know that you must conquer it through ages, centuries— must pay for it with a proportionate price. For you too, as for all lands, the struggle, the traitor, the wily person in office, scrofulous wealth, the surfeit of prosperity, the demonism of greed, the hell of passion, the decay of faith, the long postponement, the fossil-like lethargy, the ceaseless need of revolutions, prophets, thunder-storms, deaths, births, new projections, and invigorations of ideas and men."

The *Memoranda during the War* is mainly a record of personal experiences, nursing the sick and wounded soldiers in the hospitals ; most of it is in a low key, simple, unwrought, like a diary kept for one's-self, but it reveals the large, tender, sympathetic soul of the poet, and puts in practical form that unprecedented and fervid comradeship which is his leading element, even more than his elaborate works. It is printed almost verbatim, just as the notes were jotted down at the time and on the spot. It is impossible to read it without the feeling of tears, while there is elsewhere no such portrayal of the common soldier, and such appreciation of him as is contained in its pages. It is heart's blood, every word of it, and along with "Drum-taps" is the only literature of the war thus far, entirely characteristic, and worthy of serious mention. There are in particular two passages in the Memoranda that have amazing dramatic power, vividness, and rapid action, like some quick painter covering a large canvas. I refer to the account of the assassination of President Lincoln, and that of the scenes in Washington after the first battle of Bull Run. What may be called the mass-movement of Whitman's prose style, the rapid marshalling and grouping together of many facts and details, gathering up, and recruiting, and expanding, as the sentences move along, till the force and momentum become like a rolling flood, or an army in échelons on the charge, is here displayed with wonderful effect.

Noting and studying what forces move the world, the only sane explanation that comes to me of the fact that such writing as these little volumes contain has not, in this country especially, met with its due recognition and approval, is, that like all Whitman's works, they have really never yet been published at all, in the true sense have never entered the arena where the great laurels are won. They have been printed by the author, and a few readers have found them out, but to all intents and purposes they are unknown.

I have not dwelt on Whitman's personal circumstances, his age (he is now, 1877, entering his 59th year), paralysis, seclusion, and the treatment of him by certain portions of the literary classes, although those have all been made the subjects of wide discussion of late, both in America and Great Britain, and have, I think, a bearing under the circumstances on his character and genius. It is an unwritten tragedy that will doubtless always remain unwritten. I will but allude to an eloquent appeal of the Scotch poet, Robert Buchanan, published in London in March 1876, eulogising and defending the American bard in his old age, illness, and poverty, from the swarms of maligners who still continue to assail him. The appeal has this fine passage :—

"He -who wanders through the solitudes of far-off Uist or lonely Donegal may often behold the Golden Eagle sick to death, worn with age or famine, or with both, passing with weary waft of wing from promontory to promontory, from peak to peak, pursued by a crowd of rooks and crows, which fall back screaming whenever the noble bird turns his indignant head, and which follow frantically once more, hooting behind him, whenever he wends again upon his way."

Skipping many things I would yet like to touch upon—for this paper is already too long—I will say in conclusion that if any reader of mine is moved by what I have here written to undertake the perusal of Leaves of Grass, or the later volume, Two Rivulets, let me yet warn him that he little suspects what is before him. Poetry in the Virgilian, Tennysonian, or Lowellian sense, it certainly is not. Just as the living form of man in its ordinary garb is less beautiful (yet more beautiful) than the marble statue; just as the living woman and child that may have sat for the model, is less beautiful (yet more so) than one of Raphael's finest madonnas,—or just as a forest of trees addresses itself less directly to the feeling of what is called art and form than the house or other edifice built from them; just as you, and the whole spirit of our current times, have been trained to feed on and enjoy, not Nature or Man, or the aboriginal forces, or the actual, but pictures, books, art, and the selected and refined— just so these poems will doubtless first shock and disappoint you. Your admiration for the beautiful is never the feeling directly and chiefly addressed in them, but your love for the breathing flesh, the concrete reality, the moving forms and shows of the universe. A man reaches and moves you, not an artist. Doubtless, too, a certain withholding and repugnance has first to be overcome, analogous to a cold sea plunge— and it is not till you experience the reaction, the after-glow, and feel the swing and surge of the strong waves, that you know what Walt Whitman's pages really are. They don't give themselves at first—like the real landscape and the sea, they are all indirections. You may have to try them many times; there is something of Nature's rudeness and forbiddingness, not only at the first, but probably always. But after you have mastered them by resigning yourself to them, there is nothing like them anywhere in literature for vital help and meaning. The poet says—

" The press of my foot to the earth springs a hundred affections,
That scorn the best I can do to relate them."

And the press of your mind to these pages will certainly start new and countless problems that poetry and art have never before touched, and that afford a perpetual stimulus and delight.

It has been said that the object of poetry and the higher forms of literature is to escape from the tyranny of the real into the freedom of the ideal,—but what is the ideal unless ballasted and weighted with the real? All these poems have a lofty ideal background; the great laws and harmonies stretch unerringly above them, and give their vista and perspective. It is because Whitman's ideal is clothed with rank materiality, as the soul is clothed with the carnal body, that his poems beget such warmth and desire in the mind, and are the reservoirs of so much power. No one can feel, more than I, how absolutely necessary it is that the facts of nature and experience be born again in the heart of the bard, and receive the baptism of the true fire before they be counted poetical; and I have no trouble on this score with the author of **Leaves of Grass**. He never fails to ascend into spiritual meanings. Indeed, the spirituality of Walt Whitman is the chief fact after all, and dominates every page he has written.

Observe that this singer and artist makes no direct attempt to be poetical, any more than he does to be melodious or rhythmical He approaches these qualities and results as it were from beneath, and always indirectly; they are drawn to him, not he to them, and if they appear absent from his page at first it is because we were looking for them in the customary places on the out side, where he never puts them, and had not yet penetrated the interiors. As many of the fowls hide their eggs by a sort of intuitive prudery and secretiveness, he always half hides, or more than half hides, his thought, his glow, his magnetism, his most golden and orbic treasures.

Finally, as those men and women respect and love Walt Whitman best who have known him longest and closest personally, the same rule will apply to **Leaves of Grass** and the later volume, **Two Rivulets**. It is indeed neither the first surface reading of those books, nor perhaps even the second or third, that will any more than prepare the student for the full assimilation of the poems. Like Nature, and like the Sciences, they suggest endless suites of chambers opening and expanding more and more, and continually.

The Codes Of Hammurabi And Moses
W. W. Davies

QTY

The discovery of the Hammurabi Code is one of the greatest achievements of archaeology, and is of paramount interest, not only to the student of the Bible, but also to all those interested in ancient history...

Religion   **ISBN:** *1-59462-338-4*   **Pages:132**

MSRP $12.95

The Theory of Moral Sentiments
Adam Smith

QTY

This work from 1749. contains original theories of conscience amd moral judgment and it is the foundation for systemof morals.

Philosophy   **ISBN:** *1-59462-777-0*   **Pages:536**

MSRP $19.95

Jessica's First Prayer
Hesba Stretton

QTY

In a screened and secluded corner of one of the many railway-bridges which span the streets of London there could be seen a few years ago, from five o'clock every morning until half past eight, a tidily set-out coffee-stall, consisting of a trestle and board, upon which stood two large tin cans with a small fire of charcoal burning under each so as to keep the coffee boiling during the early hours of the morning when the work-people were thronging into the city on their way to their daily toil...

Childrens   **ISBN:** *1-59462-373-2*

Pages:84

MSRP $9.95

My Life and Work
Henry Ford

QTY

Henry Ford revolutionized the world with his implementation of mass production for the Model T automobile. Gain valuable business insight into his life and work with his own auto-biography... "We have only started on our development of our country we have not as yet, with all our talk of wonderful progress, done more than scratch the surface. The progress has been wonderful enough but..."

Biographies/   **ISBN:** *1-59462-198-5*

Pages:300

MSRP $21.95

The Art of Cross-Examination
Francis Wellman

QTY

I presume it is the experience of every author, after his first book is published upon an important subject, to be almost overwhelmed with a wealth of ideas and illustrations which could readily have been included in his book, and which to his own mind, at least, seem to make a second edition inevitable. Such certainly was the case with me; and when the first edition had reached its sixth impression in five months, I rejoiced to learn that it seemed to my publishers that the book had met with a sufficiently favorable reception to justify a second and considerably enlarged edition. ...

Pages:412

Reference   **ISBN: *1-59462-647-2***   *MSRP $19.95*

On the Duty of Civil Disobedience
Henry David Thoreau

QTY

Thoreau wrote his famous essay, On the Duty of Civil Disobedience, as a protest against an unjust but popular war and the immoral but popular institution of slave-owning. He did more than write—he declined to pay his taxes, and was hauled off to gaol in consequence. Who can say how much this refusal of his hastened the end of the war and of slavery ?

Law   **ISBN: *1-59462-747-9***   **Pages:48**
MSRP $7.45

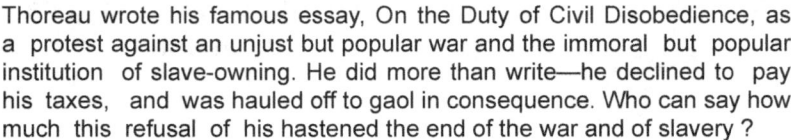

Dream Psychology Psychoanalysis for Beginners
Sigmund Freud

QTY

Sigmund Freud, born Sigismund Schlomo Freud (May 6, 1856 - September 23, 1939), was a Jewish-Austrian neurologist and psychiatrist who co-founded the psychoanalytic school of psychology. Freud is best known for his theories of the unconscious mind, especially involving the mechanism of repression; his redefinition of sexual desire as mobile and directed towards a wide variety of objects; and his therapeutic techniques, especially his understanding of transference in the therapeutic relationship and the presumed value of dreams as sources of insight into unconscious desires.

Pages:196

Psychology   **ISBN: *1-59462-905-6***   *MSRP $15.45*

The Miracle of Right Thought
Orison Swett Marden

QTY

Believe with all of your heart that you will do what you were made to do. When the mind has once formed the habit of holding cheerful, happy, prosperous pictures, it will not be easy to form the opposite habit. It does not matter how improbable or how far away this realization may see, or how dark the prospects may be, if we visualize them as best we can, as vividly as possible, hold tenaciously to them and vigorously struggle to attain them, they will gradually become actualized, realized in the life. But a desire, a longing without endeavor, a yearning abandoned or held indifferently will vanish without realization.

Pages:360

Self Help   **ISBN: *1-59462-644-8***   *MSRP $25.45*

The Rosicrucian Cosmo-Conception Mystic Christianity *by Max Heindel*　　ISBN: 1-59462-188-8　**$38.95**
The Rosicrucian Cosmo-conception is not dogmatic, neither does it appeal to any other authority than the reason of the student. It is: not controversial but is: sent forth in the, hope that it may help to clear...　　New Age/Religion Pages 646

Abandonment To Divine Providence *by Jean-Pierre de Caussade*　　ISBN: 1-59462-228-0　**$25.95**
"The Rev. Jean Pierre de Caussade was one of the most remarkable spiritual writers of the Society of Jesus in France in the 18th Century. His death took place at Toulouse in 1751. His works have gone through many editions and have been republished...　　Inspirational/Religion Pages 400

Mental Chemistry *by Charles Haanel*　　ISBN: 1-59462-192-6　**$23.95**
Mental Chemistry allows the change of material conditions by combining and appropriately utilizing the power of the mind. Much like applied chemistry creates something new and unique out of careful combinations of chemicals the mastery of mental chemistry...　　New Age Pages 354

The Letters of Robert Browning and Elizabeth Barret Barrett 1845-1846 vol II　　ISBN: 1-59462-193-4　**$35.95**
by Robert Browning and Elizabeth Barrett　　Biographies Pages 596

Gleanings In Genesis (volume I) *by Arthur W. Pink*　　ISBN: 1-59462-130-6　**$27.45**
Appropriately has Genesis been termed "the seed plot of the Bible" for in it we have, in germ form, almost all of the great doctrines which are afterwards fully developed in the books of Scripture which follow...　　Religion/Inspirational Pages 420

The Master Key *by L. W. de Laurence*　　ISBN: 1-59462-001-6　**$30.95**
In no branch of human knowledge has there been a more lively increase of the spirit of research during the past few years than in the study of Psychology, Concentration and Mental Discipline. The requests for authentic lessons in Thought Control, Mental Discipline and...　　New Age/Business Pages 422

The Lesser Key Of Solomon Goetia *by L. W. de Laurence*　　ISBN: 1-59462-092-X　**$9.95**
This translation of the first book of the "Lemegton" which is now for the first time made accessible to students of Talismanic Magic was done, after careful collation and edition, from numerous Ancient Manuscripts in Hebrew, Latin, and French...　　New Age/Occult Pages 92

Rubaiyat Of Omar Khayyam *by Edward Fitzgerald*　　ISBN: 1-59462-332-5　**$13.95**
Edward Fitzgerald, whom the world has already learned, in spite of his own efforts to remain within the shadow of anonymity, to look upon as one of the rarest poets of the century, was born at Bredfield, in Suffolk, on the 31st of March, 1809. He was the third son of John Purcell...　　Music Pages 172

Ancient Law *by Henry Maine*　　ISBN: 1-59462-128-4　**$29.95**
The chief object of the following pages is to indicate some of the earliest ideas of mankind, as they are reflected in Ancient Law, and to point out the relation of those ideas to modern thought.　　Religion/History Pages 452

Far-Away Stories *by William J. Locke*　　ISBN: 1-59462-129-2　**$19.45**
"Good wine needs no bush, but a collection of mixed vintages does. And this book is just such a collection. Some of the stories I do not want to remain buried for ever in the museum files of dead magazine-numbers an author's not unpardonable vanity..."　　Fiction Pages 272

Life of David Crockett *by David Crockett*　　ISBN: 1-59462-250-7　**$27.45**
"Colonel David Crockett was one of the most remarkable men of the times in which he lived. Born in humble life, but gifted with a strong will, an indomitable courage, and unremitting perseverance. .　　Biographies/New Age Pages 424

Lip-Reading *by Edward Nitchie*　　ISBN: 1-59462-206-X　**$25.95**
Edward B. Nitchie, founder of the New York School for the Hard of Hearing, now the Nitchie School of Lip-Reading, Inc, wrote "LIP-READING Principles and Practice". The development and perfecting of this meritorious work on lip-reading was an undertaking...　　How-to Pages 400

A Handbook of Suggestive Therapeutics, Applied Hypnotism, Psychic Science　　ISBN: 1-59462-214-0　**$24.95**
by Henry Munro　　Health/New Age/Health/Self-help Pages 376

A Doll's House: and Two Other Plays *by Henrik Ibsen*　　ISBN: 1-59462-112-8　**$19.95**
Henrik Ibsen created this classic when in revolutionary 1848 Rome. Introducing some striking concepts in playwriting for the realist genre, this play has been studied the world over.　　Fiction/Classics/Plays 308

The Light of Asia *by sir Edwin Arnold*　　ISBN: 1-59462-204-3　**$13.95**
In this poetic masterpiece, Edwin Arnold describes the life and teachings of Buddha. The man who was to become known as Buddha to the world was born as Prince Gautama of India but he rejected the world's riches and abandoned the reigns of power when...　　Religion/History/Biographies Pages 170

The Complete Works of Guy de Maupassant *by Guy de Maupassant*　　ISBN: 1-59462-157-8　**$16.95**
"For days and days, nights and nights, I had dreamed of that first kiss which was to consecrate our engagement, and I knew not on what spot I should put my lips..."　　Fiction/Classics Pages 240

The Art of Cross-Examination *by Francis L. Wellman*　　ISBN: 1-59462-309-0　**$26.95**
Written by a renowned trial lawyer, Wellman imparts his experience and uses case studies to explain how to use psychology to extract desired information through questioning.　　How-to/Science/Reference Pages 408

Answered or Unanswered? *by Louisa Vaughan*　　ISBN: 1-59452-248-5　**$10.95**
Miracles of Faith in China　　Religion Pages 112

The Edinburgh Lectures on Mental Science (1909) *by Thomas*　　ISBN: 1-59452-008-3　**$11.95**
This book contains the substance of a course of lectures recently given by the writer in the Queen Street Hall, Edinburgh. Its purpose is to indicate the Natural Principles governing the relation between Mental Action and Material Conditions...　　New Age/Psychology Pages 148

Ayesha *by H. Rider Haggard*　　ISBN: 1-59452-301-5　**$24.95**
Verily and indeed it is the unexpected that happens! Probably if there was one person upon the earth from whom the Editor of this, and of a certain previous history, did not expect to hear again...　　Classics Pages 380

Ayala's Angel *by Anthony Trollope*　　ISBN: 1-59462-352-X　**$29.95**
The two girls were both pretty, but Lucy who was twenty-one who supposed to be simple and comparatively unattractive, whereas Ayala was credited, as her Bombwhat romantic name might show, with poetic charm and a taste for romance. Ayala when her father died was nineteen...　　Fiction Pages 484

The American Commonwealth *by James Bryce*　　ISBN: 1-59452-286-8　**$34.45**
An interpretation of American democratic political theory. It examines political mechanics and society from the perspective of Scotsman James Bryce　　Politics Pages 572

Stories of the Pilgrims *by Margaret P. Pumphrey*　　ISBN: 1-59452-116-0　**$17.95**
This book explores pilgrims religious oppression in England as well as their escape to Holland and eventual crossing to America on the Mayflower, and their early days in New England...　　History Pages 268

QTY

The Fasting Cure *by Sinclair Upton*   ISBN: *1-59462-222-1*   **$13.95**
In the Cosmopolitan Magazine for May, 1910, and in the Contemporary Review (London) for April, 1910, I published an article dealing with my experiences in fasting. I have written a great many magazine articles, but never one which attracted so much attention... New Age/Self Help/Health Pages 164

Hebrew Astrology *by Sepharial*   ISBN: *1-59462-308-2*   **$13.45**
In these days of advanced thinking it is a matter of common observation that we have left many of the old landmarks behind and that we are now pressing forward to greater heights and to a wider horizon than that which represented the mind-content of our progenitors... Astrology Pages 144

Thought Vibration or The Law of Attraction in the Thought World   ISBN: *1-59462-127-6*   **$12.95**

by William Walker Atkinson   Psychology/Religion Pages 144

Optimism *by Helen Keller*   ISBN: *1-59462-108-X*   **$15.95**
Helen Keller was blind, deaf, and mute since 19 months old, yet famously learned how to overcome these handicaps, communicate with the world, and spread her lectures promoting optimism. An inspiring read for everyone... Biographies/Inspirational Pages 84

Sara Crewe *by Frances Burnett*   ISBN: *1-59462-360-0*   **$9.45**
In the first place, Miss Minchin lived in London. Her home was a large, dull, tall one, in a large, dull square, where all the houses were alike, and all the sparrows were alike, and where all the door-knockers made the same heavy sound... Childrens/Classic Pages 88

The Autobiography of Benjamin Franklin *by Benjamin Franklin*   ISBN: *1-59462-135-7*   **$24.95**
The Autobiography of Benjamin Franklin has probably been more extensively read than any other American historical work, and no other book of its kind has had such ups and downs of fortune. Franklin lived for many years in England, where he was agent... Biographies/History Pages 332

Name	
Email	
Telephone	
Address	
City, State ZIP	

☐ **Credit Card**   ☐ **Check / Money Order**

Credit Card Number	
Expiration Date	
Signature	

Please Mail to: Book Jungle
                    PO Box 2226
                    Champaign, IL 61825
or Fax to: 630-214-0564

ORDERING INFORMATION

web*: www.bookjungle.com*
email*: sales@bookjungle.com*
fax*: 630-214-0564*
mail*: Book Jungle PO Box 2226 Champaign, IL 61825*
or PayPal *to sales@bookjungle.com*

Please contact us for bulk discounts

DIRECT-ORDER TERMS

**20% Discount if You Order
Two or More Books**
Free Domestic Shipping!
Accepted: Master Card, Visa,
Discover, American Express